"Messages of Hope"

In this book we are encouraged to reject our fears and overcome the tensions sustained and amplified by this unbalanced and chaotic world that too easily defines and constrains us from being what we can become. One message says it plainly--get off the merry-go-round and get on the merry-go-forward! Judith as a leader brings this into clear focus. Judith as a healer channels essential energies into caring for our bodies, minds, hearts and spirits. A living life is dynamic and open. To be present and engaged and peaceful and merry, we must choose love and joy and balance and harmony, and we must receive light and life and energy and power. Judith earnestly wants us to catch and surf good waves, resonating with and amplifying them moment to moment. This is real wisdom.
　—Glenn Jones, B.Sc., M.D., F.R.C.P.C., M.Sc. - Antigua and Barbuda

Judith has accomplished what most in the spiritual community dream of, to live a life in connection with a higher order, receive those divine truths and then, most importantly, take that deep breath and share them with the world. The insights offered by "US", are always timely, profound and insightful. They reach to the very core of each of us and remind us of who we really can be. It is fitting that this body of work is shared now, during of one of the most deeply spiritual times in our history. Thank you Judith.
　—Mark Daniel, Shaman and Spiritual Guide, Ottawa

Each message that "US" delivers is profound on so many levels and reaches to the core of your being shifting discordant energy to a higher vibration. Judith and "US" are here to support you on your life's journey and to guide you to be in the flow, and in harmony with yourself, others and your environment. These words have given me an immense sense of inner peace and hope for all of us on this planet, and the Universe we live in. It is such amazing information and I am excited for it to get out there!
　—Sandra Kirkpatrick, Retired Medical Lab Technologist, Vancouver

Judith Onley is an extremely gifted Intuitive Channel, who has acted as a Spiritual Mentor to me since 2009. As a clear conduit for "Messages of Hope" from "US", the United Souls of Heaven and Earth, Judith has been an inspiration to those who have been called to entrain with her. These Divine messages are catalysts for awakening for individuals who are consciously on the Path of Ascension, and consistently remind us of the truth of who we really are!

—Chrissy Cook, International Speaker and
Best-Selling Author, Connecticut

Allow the Words in "Messages of Hope" to filter in, to and through you, for each word IS Lighted Activation. Timeless Words of Truth, Wisdom, Love, Joy and Gratitude are found within the pages of this Book. Read it chronological order, or simply allow the page you need to find you! The Words embodied Within Have Been, Are, and Always Will Be Relevant and Applicable to Your Life, supporting All Life through Spiritual Evolution and Growth!

—Alisa "RavenHeart" Liverance, Vibrational Healer,
Guide and Empath, Ontario

Judith Onley is a very clear channel for "US" (United Souls Of Heaven and Earth) to share their messages through. The information given is a vibrational roadmap of insights, guidance and soul-utions in which to navigate our lives, no matter what is going on within us and around us. This is a must read book for any spiritual being having a human incarnation!

—Kelly McCormick, Intuitively Guided Business Growth
and Marketing, California

These Light Beings, simply known as "US", give us an ever clearer picture of mankind's destiny and reminds us of who we really are," Divine Spirit in Love and Service." Thank you Judith for your service to humanity.

—Montserrat Bastus, Director, El Manantial Centre,
Santes Creus, Spain

Judith, with divine support, has gifted us with a book of love, light and hope at a time when our earthly situation may seem quite the opposite. She reminds us to experience the miracle that we, our lives and our planet are, and perceive the beauty that pervades everything, including ourselves.

—Hyla Cass MD, author of *8 Weeks to Vibrant Health*
(www.cassmd.com), California

I am profoundly grateful and honoured to have experienced first-hand the transformational energy of "US" (United Souls of Heaven and Earth). Whether live in person or through teleconference channels, I have felt a deep and awe-inspiring sense that I am in the presence of powerful and loving beings. Each channel has affected me in a different way, both physically and spiritually, but every time I feel a shift towards greater understanding of myself and the divinely supported journey we are all undertaking. If you are ready to seek true understanding and spiritual growth I recommend you start here, with Judith and "US".

—Jen Clarke,
Administrative Assistant, Toronto

The overwhelming experience I have when reading these messages is one of 'being in conversation with…'. Judith has been able to share communication that is reciprocal, where we ourselves are invited to take part as we read/listen and attune to the words of "US". Clarity and truth animate these messages, reminding us that we are, in essence, Love and there is nothing to do but to remember that simple truth. Thank you to Judith and "US" for continuing to share wisdom and reassurance through the channeled teachings.

— M. Purves, B.A., L.C.H., M.A.R.H.,
Cambridge, England

Messages of Hope from "Us"
(United Souls of Heaven and Earth)

Decade of Light — Volume 1

Through Judith Onley

FriesenPress

Suite 300 - 990 Fort St
Victoria, BC, V8V 3K2
Canada

www.friesenpress.com

Copyright © 2017 by Judith Onley
First Edition — 2017

Cover Design by Eric D. Groleau
Judith's Photo by Denise Foxwell

All rights reserved.

No part of this publication may be reproduced in any form, or by any means, electronic or mechanical, including photocopying, recording, or any information browsing, storage, or retrieval system, without permission in writing from FriesenPress.

ISBN
978-1-5255-0524-9 (Hardcover)
978-1-5255-0525-6 (Paperback)
978-1-5255-0526-3 (eBook)

1. BODY, MIND & SPIRIT

Distributed to the trade by The Ingram Book Company

Dedication

To all those beautiful beings who are embracing their journey in this life with dedication and trust, knowing that there is so much more for all of us yet to experience: may the messages in this book support you and inspire you to continue that journey with joy, enthusiasm, and a deep knowing of your truth as a Divine Being on this Earth.

TABLE OF CONTENTS

Praise for
"Messages of Hope" i

Dedication vii

Note To Readers xiii

Introduction xv

DECADE OF LIGHT 1

Influencing Others 3

Light Waves and Energy 5

Alignment of Energies 7

Love and Light... Conscious Intent 11

The Descension of Energy 13

Just Love 15

Inner Peace Creates Outer Peace 17

Worthiness 19

The Grounding of Love Energy 21

Success 23

Joyful Participation 25

Your Capabilities in the Universe 27

The Year of Miracles 29

Creating Instead of Working	31
The Next Wave… Unity	33
Let Light and Love In	35
New Vibrations	37
Shifting, Shifting, Shifting	39
Supportive Energies	41
Merging Heaven on Earth	43
Moving Forward	45
Transformation at a Cellular Level	47
What's New Since 11-11-11?	49
Celebrating the New You in the New World	51
Embracing 2012	53
Integrating Crystal Energy	55
Vibrational Upgrade	57
Your Essence Is Blossoming	59
Clearing Discordant Energies	61
Navigating Through the Intensities	63
The "Energy" of Joy	65
Energy Sensitivities	67
Heightened Awareness	69
Dimensional Doorways	71
Alignment of Energies	73
Hold Your Sacred Space… 12-12-12 *Activation at* 12:12 *p.m.*	75

Breathe Your Light… 12-21-12 Activation	81
Moving into the Year 2013… What Now?	87
Benefiting from The New Energies	89
Being Cocooned	91
New Energy Concepts Being Integrated	93
Going with the Flow with Ease	95
Opening Up to More	97
Living in the New Energy	99
Energetic Groundwork Being Laid	101
Being in the Flow of Who You Are	103
Emanating Your Mastery of the Light	105
Staying Balanced in an Unbalanced World	109
Transitions, Changes and the Unknown	111
Wrapping Up the Old and Beginning the New	113
Perception of Energy	115
Do You REALLY Want More Joy?	117
Adaptability in the New Energies	119
Accelerated Transmutation Phase	123
Change Takes Courage	125
You Have What It Takes!	127
Truth Takes Courage	129
Emotional Balance in Unsettled Energies	131
Unsettled Energies Are Catalysts For Change	133

Tension Can Create Spiritual Growth	135
Shifting Old Energy	137
Conscious Creation	139
Are You Feeling the Shift?	143
Energies Coursing Through Your Bodies	145
The Light Stirs It Up!	149
Holding Your Light in Your New Reality	153
Acclimatizing to Higher Frequency Energies	155
Energetic Adjustments Being Made	157
Do You Believe in Unlimited Possibilities?	159
More Light Coming to Your Earth	161
New Vistas Are Arising	163
Standing on Higher Ground	165
Your Perceptions Are Changing	167
Wrap Up 2015 with Love, Embrace 2016 with JOY!	169
Epilogue	171
Acknowledgements	173
About The Author	175

Messages of HOPE from "US" (United Souls of Heaven and Earth)

Note To Readers

We are *all* Divine Beings, and the sooner we embrace this truth the quicker our world will be all that we hope it will be — a place where all human beings live in peace and harmony with one another and the environment. There are many ways to connect with this truth about ourselves, and "US" (United Souls of Heaven and Earth) gives you, the reader, the opportunity to feel the resonance of who YOU truly are. As you read the words of the messages, they will strike a chord with you that will affect you at a very deep level, a level of knowing and remembering. The words in these messages are activations at a cellular level to facilitate that remembering.

It is with great honour and humility that I share the wisdom and the energy of "US" with you.

With much love and gratitude

Judith

To learn more about the teachings from "US" go to
www.judithonley.com

Messages of HOPE from "US" (United Souls of Heaven and Earth)

Introduction

Well, I must say, I had no idea that one day I would be sitting at my computer, looking out on Lake Superior, writing a book about me channeling a group of non-physical spiritual teachers! And here I sit doing just that. It is very humbling and invigorating all at the same time to be putting this book together. What a journey it has been to get to this point of acceptance and allowing.

It all began the day I was born (I am being funny, though I know that is actually the truth). How I became aware of this gift and opportunity was actually a birth as well. About twenty years ago, around 1996, I started journaling inspirational thoughts and called it "angel writing." I knew I was being "guided" because the inspiration came through in one complete stream for a couple of pages and then would just stop like the switch got turned off. When I would read what I wrote, I was very touched at the profound beauty and wisdom that was on the page. I knew it wasn't me creating the words as they were written with a very different "personality" than my own. I am quite intense and serious, and the writings were very light, joyous, playful and, sometimes, downright comical and teasing.

It became my Sunday morning ritual to sit with my tea, enjoy the quiet, and write a couple of pages, which always made me feel wonderful—like I was in a very sacred energy. However, I have to admit, there were times when I was in great resistance, because

I went through phases of being disillusioned with "Spirit." These were times when I was just not able to make sense out of what was happening to me in my life, or in the world. Still, I kept all the writings in a binder and would refer to them often. The messages were very personal to me, and encouraged me to let go of my fear, to allow myself to experience my joy, and more. Some days I could take it all into my mind and totally "get it," and on other days I just could not. On the days when I could not, I felt like it was all just a big fairytale, a mind game I was playing with myself to make me feel better to motivate myself to have hope for the future. I understand now that I was being prepared to share these messages.

I continued to write until one day I finished by signing "U.S." which made me wonder, *What is the United States doing talking to me?* As time went on, I began writing "In Love and Service, U.S.," which eventually became "In Love and Service, Your Council of Light", and signed themselves as "US". I knew at a very deep level that it was the truth and that something extraordinary was happening. A few years earlier, while I was in meditation, I had a vision of a council of Light Beings in a magnificent temple. They were pillars of beautiful magenta light, and I had the experience of them surrounding me and being there for me with their wisdom and their support. Could this have been the Council of Light?

So I continued my Sunday morning ritual, always feeling the joyful energy and the profound sacredness of what was happening, until the spring of 2006, when I noticed the writings had changed. They were not so much about me anymore, but instead started becoming more specific to certain situations, events, or people. As always, the messages were profound and empowering.

I decided to share my experience (what I came to understand as "channeling") with a few people who were connected to the subject matter in the writings. They were profoundly touched by the words, which helped to authenticate it all for me and make it feel more *real*. It gave me comfort and trust in what was occurring within me. Then one evening in May, I was listening to an Internet broadcast of a gifted woman, Dr. Meg Blackburn Losey, who was channeling inspiring messages. As I listened, I was "told" in no uncertain terms that it was now time for me to speak my messages to live audiences. The messages were not just for me anymore. In fact, the world was waiting for me and these messages. Again, I knew it was the truth; I just did not know *how* to share them. And then I was "told" to just invite people to gatherings and speak.

Well, *that* put me into quite a tailspin, with a myriad of "what if's." What if no one came? What if nothing came out of my mouth? What if I was just making it up? What if they criticized and condemned me? What if all the years of trust and integrity I had created in my business and personal relationships went down the drain? On and on it went—until I released all the doubt and accepted at the core of my being that I had to try it and be open to whatever would happen. So I invited two friends that I knew would love me anyway, no matter what happened.

I turned on the tape recorder, got all of us centred using breathing exercises and an invocation that I had received as a "download" from Spirit, and we sat for a few moments in quiet. All of a sudden I could feel great joy come over me. I felt a beautiful smile on my face as the words "Dear Ones" came out of my mouth, and away I went speaking for about thirty minutes. Then, like in the writing, it just stopped, and "US" parted with words of great gratitude for having had the opportunity to share their words and energy. It took me a few minutes to "come back" and be present in the room with my two friends. It had been like being in a dream. My eyes had been closed the whole time, and even though I was aware of talking, when I opened my eyes, I could not really remember what

I said. However, my two friends sure did, and they were in awe. As they shared the powerful affect this experience had on them, I knew it was real and was so grateful they had been willing subjects.

Because of this, my confidence increased greatly. The next time I invited four friends, and the experience was the same for them, as well as for me. Then "US" told me it was important to hold gatherings on June 6, 2006, as the 666 alignment had been interpreted with much untruth and fear. So I did a channeling with one friend at 6:00 a.m. on the beach out in front of my house. Later, eleven personally selected people showed up for a gathering at 6:00 p.m. in my house. The channel and the reflections through discussion afterward were again profound and powerful, and I knew it had made a great difference in the lives of those who had gathered in my home.

It astonished me how people just showed up by someone passing my email invitation on to them, such as Kevin, who "resonated" with what he read, and called to attend. As a result of attending my live channel, Kevin had a profound spiritual experience that he has continued to deepen and share with others through his music, and his own teachings. He became my accompanist and brought through beautiful music that he either played on the piano or sang with his angelic voice, touching the hearts and souls of those in the room.

Many people who were inspired to come to these channels also facilitated opportunities to share the messages from "US" in other locations in Toronto, such as New Thought Churches, and the St. Lawrence Centre for the Arts. The St. Lawrence Centre is a beautiful theatre in downtown Toronto, filled with the energies of dance and music and performance, which being a dancer teacher in my previous career, touched me deeply and intensified the *joy* I felt while in the presence of "US" in that particular venue. From then on, I have been open to guidance to understand when and where to offer the teachings and wisdom of this wonderful group of non-physical spiritual teachers who call themselves "US" (being glad they shortened the abbreviation from "U.S."). This openness and trust has taken me on incredible traveling adventures throughout Canada, United States, Mexico and Europe, connecting me with like-hearted people. I am honoured, grateful, and in awe of the presence of "US" in my life. I move forward with complete trust, knowing we are all meant to be of service in ways that may not make sense at first, but prove to transcend anything we can imagine.

Who is "US"?

"US" (United Souls of Heaven and Earth) is a group of loving, supportive, non-physical spiritual teachers whose purpose for coming through to us at this time is just as their name indicates:

"To unite Heaven and Earth by activating the Divine Essence within all Human Beings."

Their wisdom and teachings are timely as we go through this unique Great Shift on Earth, which parallels our own personal spiritual awakening. The channeled words spoken are not only empowering messages, but also activations of our Light at a deep cellular level. This allows us as human beings to *feel* our Divine Essence from within, thereby enabling us to integrate it fully into our every thought, word, and action of our daily lives, creating Heaven on Earth here and now!

The vibration emanating from "US" is of true joy and love, which is intensely felt by all who have been in their presence. They give us this experience of the *energy* of joy and love in our physical bodies so we can remember it as we move through our everyday lives.

through Judith Onley

What is Channeling?

Channeling is a gateway between the physical and non-physical realms facilitated through a human being who is willing to speak the words for all to benefit from the teachings and wisdom of the higher realms of enlightenment. It is a blending of these energies for the betterment of humankind through awareness and empowerment.

A Note on How the Messages Are Delivered

Embedded within the words of the messages you are about to read is a harmonic coding. There is an energetic patterning, cadence, and flow of the sentences that facilitates an activation, not necessarily at the cognitive level, though more importantly at the cellular level.

As you read the words simply allow yourself to *feel* the beautiful vibration that these messages bring to us and through us. They remind us that we truly are the conduits of Light on our Earth at this time of incredible change in consciousness.

You will hear and *feel* this cadence even more in the audio recordings of the channels. If you listen to the audio recordings you will hear clicking, clapping, and tapping sounds. This is "US" working through me, clearing energy by having me snap my fingers, clap my hands, and tap my body in different places. Audio recordings of channels from "US" are available at www.judithonley.com/products.

Much energy work is done with each of you through the words and sounds, whether you are with me in person, listening to the channels at a later date, or reading the messages in my books. It is all in the "now" moment, and you will receive the energy and activations whenever you read or listen to these empowering messages that "US" has been transmitting through me for over ten years.

This book is not meant to be read like a novel that you cannot put down. By reading each chapter one at a time, and then taking quiet time afterward to allow the words and energy to filter down from your mind to be embodied at the heart level, you will receive the activations that are encoded in the words more fully. While reading you may experience drowsiness or tingling which is a sign that you are integrating the energy at a cellular level. Taking a nap or reading this book before you go to bed will enhance that process as it takes your mind out of the equation to allow the integration to happen more quickly and with greater ease.

Another way to "receive" the energy contained in these beautiful messages is to get yourself centred, open the book to a random page and read the words, sentences or paragraphs that stand out. You will be amazed at how relevant they are to what is happening for you in the moment!

You are about to embark on an incredible journey of love, joy and empowerment through the beautiful words and energy of "US". Enjoy!

Messages of HOPE from "US" (United Souls of Heaven and Earth)

DECADE OF LIGHT
December 31, 2009

Dearest Beautiful Beings of Light,

As you come to completion with the year 2009, a year of integration of Mastery energy, you are moving into a new "Decade of Light" unprecedented on your Earth. This past year was about much transition, completion, and integration. The year 2010 heralds the beginning of a whole new harmonics of vibration of the Light from within you. The amplification of all your personal gifts in whatever medium your choose to express them will be very noticeable and applicable. There has been much preparation work done energetically on all levels for this next stage of your evolution, so rejoice in that knowing, share it with others, and celebrate! Celebrate and acknowledge those gifts in yourself and all who you connect with.

Those who stand before you and interact in your life in this coming year will emanate a love and radiance that will be breathtaking . . . and you are one of them. That is why we refer to you as Light Beings; that is not only what you are but who you are. You are the angels who have come to Earth at this time to *be* the light, not just read about it or talk about it, but to live it and breathe it. The proverbial "light bulb" moments will literally become the norm. You have shed so much density and negativity in the past decade that you will now truly experience your lightness within your physical body. You will actually see it in others with your physical eyes, not just your inner vision.

The depictions in your beautiful artwork of the glow around Celestial Beings are not fantasy or a product of your imagination. The glow is very real, and now you all have the physical capacity to clearly see it and emanate it. Your scientists and physicists are doing much to substantiate this phenomenon, thereby making it more accepted in your mainstream world (not just within your spiritual communities), because your scientists are looked upon as having credibility and will reach those who need that validation. They have come as scientists into this realm at this time to substantiate the spiritual and metaphysical events that will occur in greater proportions in this decade.

We have called this the "Decade of Light" because you have truly moved through the darkness and can embrace and embody your Light, anytime you so choose, with ease and grace. There is much support from the Celestial and Cosmic realms for you to do so. Sing your song, dance your dance, create your art, write your book, do whatever feeds your soul, and infuse all you do with your Light and your love. Emanate your luminosity and light up your world with *joy*!

Messages of HOPE from "US" (United Souls of Heaven and Earth)

Influencing Others
January 21, 2010

Dearest Beautiful Beings of Light,

Are you aware of how you influence others in your day-to day-life? Not just with suggestions you may make to them or things you may "teach" them, but actually influencing them energetically? Just standing beside a person influences them. Looking at a person influences them, especially if it is direct contact with the eyes, as then it reaches a soul level. Thinking about a person influences them and has a very beneficial impact on them if it is done with love. If there is a person or situation in your life that feels difficult or challenging, think of them with thoughts of love and you will feel the energy transform. Look at them physically with the eyes of love and watch them lighten up. Touch them with the hands of love (even if it is only in your imagination) and you will feel them soften. And, most importantly, speak to them with words of love, and experience any tension or difficultly that may have been between you melt away.

This applies to your own selves as well. What we have just shared with you is only relevant and effectual if you have applied it to yourself first. Do you think of yourself with thoughts of love? Do you look at yourself with eyes of love? Do you touch yourself with the caring hands of love and compassion? And most importantly, do you speak to yourself with words of love and experience your own tension melt away? Influencing others can be done in many ways, either to create harmony or separation. If it is to be effective in creating harmony in your world, it must come from a deep inner knowing, acknowledgement, and exuding of your love and your Light! Shine your Light on others as we have just described, and watch how quickly things will transform for both yourself and those you care about.

It does not take a lot of work—just a conscious choice in each moment that then becomes the new program, your new way of being. Your life will become so much richer on all levels, and this is how you make a difference. This is how you change the world. This is how you create Heaven on Earth right now, right here in this moment, and the next and the next. It is a minute-by-minute process that affects the whole grand scheme of the Universe. You *are* that powerful! You are Divine Beings here at this time for this purpose, so embrace the vibration of love, and send it forth in all the ways we have spoken of.

Messages of HOPE from "US" (United Souls of Heaven and Earth)

Light Waves and Energy
February 22, 2010

Dearest Beautiful Beings of Light,

We have said that 2010 will be the heralding of the Decade of Light and that much will happen in this year that has been, to this point, beyond your comprehension; many of you are now starting to experience it. There is much talk in metaphysical circles about *Light*, and there are many variations in how it is defined and described and used. You are now experiencing greater amplification of Light, of your Light, and it is coming in waves. Your body is a very delicate, intricate, and complex instrument that needs to be handled with great love and care during these times of transition from its third-dimensional density to its *Lightness*. It is an intense process that requires awareness and tuning in. You are not only receiving intense Light waves and energy from the Universe; you are now also emanating them on a more consistent basis, so there is a 'harmony without' that is being created from the 'harmony within.' Harmony is being created, even though it feels quite unsettling for most of you at this time. And it is coming and going in waves as the density is dissolved. That is why one day you feel splendid and the next day like a truck has hit you.

With each wave of Light and energy that you receive from the Cosmos, there is an integration time to allow your 'physicalness' to adjust; it is important to rest during these periods. It is during your rest times that much of the work to upgrade your systems can be done so you are then able to feel so much joy and bliss on a grander scale and to exude that to all in your presence, as well as through your thoughts. As you embrace this process with a deep knowing of the profundity of what is happening on your Earth and in your bodies at this magnificent intersection of time and energies, you will *feel* your own Light and energy. It will become the everyday norm, not just a concept or something for avatars, yogis and Masters. You are the Masters now. You are the embodiment of the Divine Source, and it is your Light from within that will shift the darkness on your Earth, that will raise the vibration, that will create a harmonic resonance for all to connect with. An analogy for you would be your gas stove. The pilot light is lit, though it is only a little flame waiting to do its job (that is the Light inside of you). Universal energy is like the match that ignites the whole burner, so it has a greater capacity to do what it is here to do. That is what is happening for you, Dear Ones: you are being ignited to operate on all burners. Dance in the flames, ride the waves, embrace the energy, and be the *Light* that you already are (on steroids)!

Messages of HOPE from "US" (United Souls of Heaven and Earth)

Alignment of Energies
March 22, 2010

Dearest Beautiful Beings of Light,

There are many things happening in your energy fields that are unbeknownst to you. These things are happening to align you with your own higher vibrational energy, which supports the truth of who you are and your expression of that truth. As you become more and more aware of your truth, these alignments will be much more beneficial to you in your ongoing, everyday lives. You will be in sync, so to speak, with all aspects of yourself and the Universe. There has been a fragmentation that you have been working with for a very long time that is now coming into alignment, because it is time, and because you are giving intention for that by opening to the *moreness* of yourself, as well as the *moreness* of the Universe. We have spoken of the *moreness* before, and we will assist you to expand your awareness of that energy in the coming months.

Along with the alignment of energy within yourself and the Universe—because the Universe is contained within your cells—comes the ease that you have so longed for. Decisions become simpler; details are carried out with acceleration, almost like magic. You will be scratching your head and saying to yourself, "How did that happen?" These alignments of energy will bring new people and situations into your life that will be like a dream come true, connecting at greater heart levels rather than intellectual levels, thus facilitating the joy in the *doingness* that will take place as a result of these connections.

We hear you ask, "How do I align with these new energies?" It is through your own thought and intention. These alignments are happening whether you are aware of them or not, so as you set your intention to be conscious of what is happening around you and how you are feeling on the inside, you are more in tune with what is aligning for you. It can be little things, like your schedule unexpectedly changing and, as a result, something even more wonderful taking place in that time-space. Or making a decision to change something you had committed to that just did not feel quite right, and then suddenly it opens space for you to do something that is much more fulfilling. It happens because you are aligned with your own truth, and when you do that, Dear Ones, it is always beneficial to the others involved, always!

So as you focus on thoughts, feelings, situations, people and energies that are in harmony with you and who you are, you are raising the vibration for not only yourself, but for your planet. That accelerates the shift that your world is currently in towards living in harmony and joy from within, thus allowing greater alignments of energy to be amplified. When this happens, it creates a resonant field in the external world of your manifestations, bringing to you many unexpected things and opportunities.

Be open to new possibilities. Know that for every so-called problem, the solution has already been created, whether it is on a personal level, global level, or Cosmic level. These alignment of energies are supporting the clearing of space for the implementation of powerful new solutions. These new solutions are energetic, broad-based, and expansive in effect. The effects are supporting you on all levels: physical, mental, emotional and spiritual, no matter

Messages of HOPE from "US" (United Souls of Heaven and Earth)

how uncomfortable it may feel in the moment. You are powerful beings, and as you embrace this alignment of energies, you will feel that power from within—and that is where it all begins!

Messages of HOPE from "US" (United Souls of Heaven and Earth)

Love and Light...
Conscious Intent
April 21, 2010

Dearest Beautiful Beings of Light,

"Love and Light": this is a term many of you use to sign off your writings, but do you really know what it means? Are you using these words (or any words, for that matter) consciously, or do they roll out of your mind because you saw them somewhere, or heard someone say them, and thought they were nice? Yes, they are nice and pretty and very New Age, but are you aware every time you use them that they are a vibration that can and do have an impact, and that impact can be amplified with your conscious intent? By being conscious of the words you speak, write, or even think, you can change your world. You can change your way of being in the world. You can lift yourself up out of the density. You can lift others up. It does not always take a physical act or action to change how things are. Much more can be accomplished with your conscious intent and awareness of what you put out in thought energy, and then to put it out into the mass consciousness with passion.

Let's take the term "Love and Light." As you sign an email, take a moment before hitting the send button to give those words some heart energy, not just perfunctory energy. It is like fertilizing your garden. If you want to have big, healthy, blossoming plants, you give them extra attention and add fertilizer. By taking a moment to give your whole-hearted intent that the person receiving that email truly receives the energy of these words, you are fertilizing not only them but yourself. You must feel it to truly be able to give it.

Conscious intent is a powerful way of being. It can move mountains. It is like adding jet fuel to your thoughts or actions. It can open hearts, and that is empowering to both the sender and the receiver. It allows more Light to be anchored on your Earth. And that is the intense transition you are all going through at this time: anchoring light through your physical bodies and expressing it through your heart, through loving thoughts and actions. Raising the vibration on your Earth, being the Light Beings you already are, and giving conscious intent to exude that Light for all to benefit is why you are here. So we encourage you to do it consciously and to do it with *joy*!

Messages of HOPE from "US" (United Souls of Heaven and Earth)

The Descension of Energy
May 12, 2010

Dearest Beautiful Beings of Light,

You are Light Beings with a capital L and a capital B. We are going to do whatever we are able through our words and through our transmission of energy to help you to have that experience, because it is in the physical form, in the biological interaction, that your Light is able to come through, that your Light is able to take action, that your Light is able to be effective.

So as we say these words to you, allow yourselves to just feel. *Feeling* is another word that we often use in our descriptions, because it is about feeling. It is not about *thinking*, Dear Ones— it is about *feeling*. It is about allowing the energy to move down into the body. Your minds have great capacity for holding information, and as women, as Divine energy, as the Divine Feminine energy, that is being amplified at the same time as it is being *descended*, not ascended.

There are so many of you who are waiting at this time for the ascension, but it is not about ascension, Dear Ones, as you have already accomplished that—it is about the descension; that is our message to you this day. It is about the decsension of information. It is about the descension of energy. It is about the descension of activations. It is about the descension of everything that you will need from this point forward in your evolution through your physical bodies, to accomplish (though *accomplish* is more of a human word than an ethereal word, but we will use it because you can relate to it) what you are here to do.

It is about the descension of your wholeness; the descension of your Spirit; the descension of your Divine Essence; the descension of your Godliness, of your Mastery. There are so many aspects to what is happening at this time for you as human beings, for you as physical beings, for you as spiritual beings, for you as Light Beings that is all coming together. It is coming together into a beautiful harmonic dance of information and energies that is then being activated to move forward in your world, and it is going to move quickly.

Messages of HOPE from "US" (United Souls of Heaven and Earth)

Just Love

June 10, 2010

Dearest Beautiful Beings of Light,

We are aware that many of you are dealing with challenging situations in your lives. When you are not sure what to do, just love! Love is the elixir that heals all. It is a powerful energy beyond human measurement. You are just now starting to tap into the magnitude of this energy source. It goes way beyond romantic love or even motherly love. It is far grander than even a mother's love, which is powerful unto its own.

If you would allow yourselves to just love anything that comes up that causes you upset—whether it's a person, a circumstance, or global situation—while you are sending it love, your body cannot hold onto the upset (or the fear) at the same time. So you are giving yourself a great gift, and your body will love you for it. The person or situation will also be uplifted just by your intention to just love. They will receive the energy, whether they are aware of it or not, and it will dissipate the upset energy for them as well.

As you apply this in your own life and situations, it will automatically emanate and reverberate out into global and Universal situations. When you intentionally send love energy to bigger things such as the Gulf oil spill, you become part of a Light matrix that is far more powerful than any undesirable situation that man can create. So we encourage you to be aware of this magnificent energy that you all carry within your minds, your bodies, and your hearts, and to just love. You will be amazed at what starts to shift in your personal life, as well as your world. As you give out, you will receive multi-fold, so be ready to receive love from all directions. Be the example; you are the ones creating the shift into peace and harmony in your world, so let it begin with you.

Messages of HOPE from "US" (United Souls of Heaven and Earth)

Inner Peace Creates Outer Peace

July 17, 2010

Dearest Beautiful Beings of Light,

It is so very vital at this time to do whatever it takes to create your own inner peace. It is not only an emotional state, but is a vibratory state that has a greater impact on your life and your world than you could ever imagine. It is a frequency of energy that is sent forth from you like a satellite beam that affects the resonance of all people and circumstances around you. If you are exuding the frequency of inner peace you are consciously contributing to the ending of all wars and conflicts on your planet. It is an entrainment that is happening through the mass consciousness that is now overriding all of the old programs and energies that have kept humans in a state of conflict.

You have the capacity within you to lift yourselves, and all those you care about, above these denser vibrations of worry, fear, anger, and hurt. You do that by allowing the clearing of your emotional stuff, a clearing that is happening whether you are aware of it or not, and making a conscious choice in each minute of the day to choose peace: peace within your mind that is processing all that it sees and hears, peace within your body that feels all the changes that are underway, and most importantly, peace in your heart, that place of all-knowing wisdom. When you tap into your heart wisdom, you will get an instant sensation that all is well; that will become the energy that will exude from you and therefore attract experiences to prove it is so.

It is all about vibration and frequency, and you can choose to tune in to what feels good or what causes your energy to diminish. It is like flipping through the channels on your television. Some programs will leave you feeling inspired and light-hearted, and others will leave you feeling worried and downcast. Which ones do you feel are serving you, Dear Ones? Anything that gives you the feeling of well-being is amplifying your ability to create peace from within. When you have peace from within, you receive inspired guidance and energy to take whatever actions are appropriate in your life to orchestrate that harmony with your loved ones. This harmony then reverberates out into the mass consciousness that affects all others on your Earth. It is a simple task, but someone has got to do it; we are so joyful to see so many of you embracing this as the focus of your personal evolution.

It is with great honour we support you energetically to feel your inner peace on a more amplified level by just reading these words and being open to the activation of your Divine Essence that lives in a constant state of inner peace.

Messages of HOPE from "US" (United Souls of Heaven and Earth)

Worthiness

August 30, 2010

Dearest Beautiful Beings of Light,

Worthiness is a topic discussed quite often in spiritual teachings, both in an empowering way and, in some of your doctrines, a rather disempowering way (i.e., "sinners"). If you accept the truth that you are truly Light Beings having a human, Earthly experience, worthiness would be a non-issue for you; however, because of misinterpreted teachings and belief systems, you have accepted a belief that you are somehow less than what you truly are.

Our purpose is to help you to release these misinterpretations, these limitations, so you can graciously acknowledge your worthiness. Your worth is not based on your education, or your financial situation, or your social status, or even the hierarchy established within your own families or cultures. Your worth is *you*! It is all the beautiful aspects of you and the gifts that you have to offer humanity because of who you are. It is intrinsic, and does not have to be earned in any way. And as you accept that fact, your own self acknowledgement, there is nothing to do to prove it. You will not need to have a long list of accomplishments to show others for them to affirm you. They will see your Light from within and honour that and want to support you in ways you could never have even imagined or thought to ask for.

Just being born on Earth has created your weight in gold—not gold bullion, which can be measured, but golden Light that could never be captured, contained, or measured. It is invaluable, as are you. No dollar amount, or any other form of measurement, can be assigned to your name (your energy signature), because it is endless. Many Lightworkers are experiencing financial struggles, Dear Ones, and that is because it is now time to experience your worth in Light quotients. Own who and what you are and worthiness will never again be a point of concern for you. Your worthiness just *is*! And it is now being activated on a grander scale for the creation of the New Earth. Feel your Light and acknowledge it in yourself, and acknowledge it in all you meet, for it is the truth and the way.

Messages of HOPE from "US" (United Souls of Heaven and Earth)

The Grounding of Love Energy

September 12, 2010

Dearest Beautiful Beings of Light,

What you are experiencing in your physical bodies is much electrical energy. It is energy that is coming from the Cosmos. It is coming from many dimensions, from many Beings as we are able to integrate and get closer to you in your Earthly realm, in your 3D realm. There is a great adjustment that has to happen for us to be able to work more fully with you, and these energies are very high vibrational, high frequency, and it is important that you ground them through your body.

Even though we are in your presence, you are the conduit. We have said this many times before: you are the conduit of the Cosmic energies. You are the conduit of the Universal energies; you are the conduit of the multi-dimensional energies; you are the conduit of all of the Light energies, because you are Light. So when you really get that, Dear Ones, that you are Light, conducting will become easier. But each time, the Light is either moving from you or to you.

So there is much work going on with your biological, chemical system for that to happen in a more easeful way. There is much,

much, much, much work going on in your emotional field right now—and to be discerning of what is yours and what is not yours as you go through these portals of old energies, such as what you just went through with your September 11th event anniversary. This is the most significant time. You are grounding such big energies at this time for your Mother Earth, for your bodies, for your species, and that is why it is so uncomfortable. If you can allow yourself to be at peace with this and not get out into the chaos, you will fare very well.

So our message to you at this time, Dear Ones, is to ground the energy of Love through your physical body. Have it start with s*elf*-Love, knowing that self-Love has no place to go but upward. Grounding the energy of Love through your physical body is what we are here to assist you with this particular day, knowing that as you do that for yourself it ripples out to everything and everyone.

Success
October 20, 2010

Dearest Beautiful Beings of Light,

How do you measure success? What does success mean to you? What does that look like in your life? Do you base it on what you perceive success looks like in other people's lives?

These are all very relevant questions at this point in your evolution, because much of what you might have based your success on is being challenged or even quickly disappearing. So we are here to help you redefine success as you start to rediscover who you truly are, and that you have unlimited access to joy and love.

Many of you felt this energy very intensely through the recent 10-10-10 alignment of energies.

The reason for your acquiring of material goods is to feel good and bring you and those around you joy, is it not? Why not go for the joy first and see what happens? Waking up in the morning with a smile on your face could be considered one of your greatest successes in times of challenge. Helping another to feel good would be way up there on the success ladder as well. There is no way to measure these two examples as they are off the Richter scale.

And isn't that fun—making everything you do in a day be off the Richter scale, gonging the bell, blowing a hole in the roof (of your beliefs)? Success, Dear Ones, is truly about feeling good. If you have created any amount of good feeling in your day, you have been successful. You do not have to have a diploma or certificate to prove it, nor a fancy car or big house or large bank account, though those things (or whatever it is you desire) are more than likely to appear from thin air as you experience more joy. Remember, it is all about vibration, and as you choose to feel good, you are immersed in the vibration of joy that can only bring you more good feelings—and it just keeps building and spiraling upwards.

So we wish you much success in all of your endeavours. May they be done with a smile on your face and joy in your heart!

Messages of HOPE from "US" (United Souls of Heaven and Earth)

Joyful Participation
November 25, 2010

Dearest Beautiful Beings of Light,

Do you experience joy in everything you do? You can, you know; it is just a matter of choice—and, we would like to add, of receiving. There is much joyful energy around you at all times, no matter what the media tries to persuade you to believe. You can experience joy in the seemingly most insignificant of circumstances or situations. You can engage in anything, whether with resistance, fear, resentment *or* with joy!

Take a look at your day. How much of your day do you truly participate in with full joy? Oh, you have your moments, though they are fleeting. Sometimes it is much easier than others. We are here to help you to anchor the energy of *joy*, to have the physical experience, to feel it in your body, to create it with your mind, to let it reverberate from you like a beautiful musical note, which has a harmonizing effect—not only on the cells of your body, but on all those around you. As you participate joyfully in your life, you are the inspiration for others to do so as well. It becomes uncontrollably contagious. What fun! You get to see and feel why you are here on Earth, to experience the *joy* of life—*your* life. Not looking through the eyes of someone else's life. This is *your* moment to experience joy.

You have chosen to be here at this time for this purpose. The sun, the moon, the stars and the planets have all aligned for this purpose. There has been much energetic support for this time you now walk in. Embrace it fully. You have orchestrated it, so enjoy the melody. As you come into this season of celebration, know that it was designed by you to celebrate one another with joy; make that your intention. There *is* joy in everything and everyone if that is what you choose to experience. Celestial Beings in all realms are singing, dancing, and laughing with you and emanating their *joy* to you so you can truly know what it feels like to receive this beautiful energy.

Messages of HOPE from "US" (United Souls of Heaven and Earth)

Your Capabilities in the Universe
December 12, 2010

Dearest Beautiful Beings of Light,

This is one of the messages that is becoming clearer to all of you now, that you understand. We are going to tie this together today with your understanding of your capabilities in the Universe, because this is something that has been hidden from you, Dear Ones. You think that you are just a human being walking around the Earth, trying to do your life and make everything work and not to have too much stress or too much trauma. As you do that, you are actually forgetting your magnificence in the Universe, your capabilities in the Universe.

It is not just on your Earth. You are on this Earth, on Mother Earth, in your 3D realm for a great purpose, and it is much grander than what you have experienced up to this point. No matter how much you have allowed yourself to open your mind, you have still kept it very limited. So it is now time for you to expand your mind so that you can expand your capabilities. It is about this expansion in the Universe. It is expansion of your spiritual energy, of your Divine energy, to be its expansive self within the Universe, which it already always has been. And now it is about your awareness of it.

So it is really in your best interest, in the highest good of all, Dear Ones, to always connect with like-hearted, conscious individuals who are ready, willing, and able to tap into the universal capabilities.

Every thought you have, every word you say, every action you take now is very exponentialized. So as you are understanding that and living in your capabilities now, your universal capabilities, then you can create anything you want. That actually sounds scary to some of you. You are picking up an energy that is almost too big for you, and we want to assure you that it is not, Dear Ones. It is not at all.

It is now time for you to fully embody your Universality. You are not just on this little planet. You encompass everything that ever was and ever will be. So as you are really having that expansion of your capabilities in the Universe, and you are feeling it, you can actually have more fun with it. Make it a game!

Messages of HOPE from "US" (United Souls of Heaven and Earth)

The Year of Miracles
January 1, 2011

Dearest Beautiful Beings of Light,

It is with great joy that we bring you these words on the eve of one of the most momentous occasions in human history. There have been many markers along the path of human evolution and enlightenment; however, this moment is one that truly will be remembered forever. When we say *this moment*, we are referring to the *here and now*, because that is where the power lies. And this moment of today, as you turn your calendars from the year 2010 to 2011, activates a numerological alignment—which *you* created many eons ago—that is now upon you. This is the marker that will show you who you are, what you as Divine Beings in a human body are truly capable of—not just on a physical or emotional level, but a meta-physical, quantum level.

In our channel on this eve last year, we spoke of how you are stepping into the Decade of Light; now you have had a year of experiencing many transitions from human thinking and being to Divine thinking and Being. Even though many of you have experienced great transitions in how you knew your life to be, you have also experienced much more of your own Light; that will increase in greater capacity in 2011.

This alignment of time and energies is giving you the quantum fuel or propulsion to move you into a time/space zone that, if you allow, will support you to bring forth the miracles that were so natural to you before the beginning of time as you know and remember it. We use the word *miracles* because that is what you can relate to and will give you hope and inspiration to embrace the totality of what you are capable of, though it is really nothing out of the ordinary; you will eventually understand that it is how you do creation on this 3D plane.

That is why you are here, and as you consciously choose love and joy, the Cosmos, the Universe, the planets and all non-seen Celestial forces are able to then fuel you and transport your physical being into that miracle zone vibration of Mastery. Our channels and activations given to you in the last two years were about *your* Mastery. Now you have cleared much of the denser energy that has kept you inhibited, and are ready to own it. So you, Dear Ones, are the ones to create the fireworks of celebration in 2011 just by being you! The energy fields have been anchored for much more acceptance of you and your path, so boldly step out and share. Share your truth, share your wisdom, share your joy and, most of all, share your love; make no exclusions.

Who you thought others were is also an illusion that will dissipate this year. There has been much emotional healing re-calibration going on for you in the Universal energy field in 2010 that will facilitate a greater capacity for acceptance of things, people, and situations that you have not understood to this point, which will now become crystal clear, as the crystal energy is being activated and amplified in your physical energy field to correspond with the Universal energy field. All that is being asked of you in this process is to stay centred and in your heart. As you do, the "light-bulb" moments will become the norm as you connect, connect, connect the dots of awareness and wisdom from within.

Messages of HOPE from "US" (United Souls of Heaven and Earth)

Creating Instead of Working

January 31, 2011

Dearest Beautiful Beings of Light,

Creating is what you do. You are born creators, and as you move out of the old paradigm of working, you will discover how much more fulfilling your lives will become. This does not mean that you will all go and quit your jobs; however, it will allow you to bring yourself to your jobs with a much different perspective and energy. It does not matter whether you are self-employed, employed by someone else, or not employed at all: you are always creating. You are creating energy. So be aware of what you are creating and eliminate the word *work* from your vocabulary.

As you do this you will feel much more ease in your body. Your body has been conditioned to *work hard,* so it is always in hyper response to that thought. What if the new thought was that you can *create easy?* Just feel your body's response to that thought. Did it sigh? Did it let go of the tension and let energy flow through? Do you feel more inspired rather than anxious? Inspiration will move you forward quickly. Think of all the situations where you say you are working at something. For example, when you are working on a project, you are creating an opportunity for a manifestation of something magnificent to come from thought form into physical reality. When you are working on your health, you are creating opportunities for well-being and vitality. When you are working on a relationship, you are creating the energy field for cooperation, intimacy, love, whatever is your desire. When you are responding to an abundance of emails, you are creating communication pathways of information and connections that can creatively affect those who receive them. You get the picture.

There is much that is changing vibrationally in your world, if you will just allow it. Allow the new way of being to flow through you to be anchored into your world. It is through you, for you, and from you. That is creation. You are now starting to create from awareness instead of default, and that creation will not feel like work. It will feel joy-filled and fun if you let it. You are a creator of creation.

Messages of HOPE from "US" (United Souls of Heaven and Earth)

The Next Wave... Unity
March 5, 2011

Dearest Beautiful Beings of Light,

The next wave is upon you—a wave of energy and consciousness moving you to the shore of unity. Over the next few weeks, you have the opportunity to ride the crest of the wave and be moved along with great momentum toward the Spring Equinox (a time of the balance of light and dark). Finding your own personal balance enables you to enjoy the thrill of the ride and to feel the wind in your hair. It is an individual ride for each of you as you find that balance of dark and light, fear and love, from within; that balance can be greatly enhanced and supported by sharing the thrill of the ride with others.

We have said this many times before: as you share your experiences, you facilitate others' awareness and acknowledgement of what is happening for them as well. When you see it as thrilling as opposed to scary, it raises your vibration and is contagious.

There is much old, dense energy being cleared from your cells and psyches, so you may have noticed weird dreams or even the feeling of a life review. This is necessary and an indication that you are clearing dense energy and emotions to hold more of your own Light. Embrace these clearings for what they are and just allow them to pass through your physical and emotional being. They are not stuck there. They only get stuck if you hold onto them. It is just energy moving, just like the wave—it must move to gain the momentum it needs to serve its purpose, and that is what is happening for you on all levels.

As you embrace what is happening in the moment and adjust your footing, you will experience a deep inner knowing that you are creating unity consciousness instead of separation and fear, because you will be living it and exuding it. You have seen wonderful examples of this unity in this past month on your Earth, and it is just a precursor of what is to come. There is no turning back. The wave moves forward. It does not go backward and neither will you. The next wave is about "all for one, and one for all," and this Universal energy will support you to live that on all levels . . . to live in unity.

Messages of HOPE from "US" (United Souls of Heaven and Earth)

Let Light and Love In
April 11, 2011

Dearest Beautiful Beings of Light,

We are speaking to the cells in your body now, not to your mind, to let your cells know that it is okay, that you do know how to do this. The old conditioning, the old patterning that has been so ingrained in you, is being cleared. You can hang onto it if you want to, if it helps you to feel better, but there will come a point when it will absolutely not help you to feel better.

As you let go and trust that your bodies are being taken care of, there is much happening that is beneficial. Even though on your 3D, human, very biological terms it doesn't feel good, it is being transformed, and that is our message for you today. There have been many things happening for people in their physical level that has been disconcerting and unsettling, and yet we have always said, Dear Ones, to pay attention to that, because your body is talking to you.

The Light that is being engaged is being amplified and exuded from your physical body, which is making the difference. It is about you *being* the Light through the physical medium that is making the difference. You do not necessarily have to take your physical body and go to do something. It is about allowing that transformation. The Light is doing that for you. So, as you are allowing this transformation to happen at the physical, cellular level, you are benefiting all of the other things that are going on around your globe and in the Universe. We always add that because it is not just about your world, though there is always that connection; our focus for our message this date is on your 3D world, as that is the one where you can have the greatest impact.

You are and do adjust, like taking a dial and fine tuning. You are adjusting the dial right now as you are going through these anchorings of the Light energy on Earth through your physical body. So when we speak about you as being "magnificent Light Beings," that is, Dear Ones, the truth. And as you are giving intention through your own physical body for that Light to pour through (but to also to receive it back), it is not about shining it out, even though it is what you do naturally. Today is about receiving it, because that is what is important for you now—to be filled back up; there is much more where you will be shining it back out, and you are! There is always this ebb and flow and rhythm to energy, and all of you are now in the phase of receiving, so just allow that receiving, because you are all very amplified Light holders, and you give it very freely, no matter what that 'it' is.

This transmission is for you to receive, because it is important that you get filled up, not just on a physical level, or an energetic level. This Cosmic filling up is happening for you as we speak. So just allow yourself to tune in and feel what it's like to be given to.

Messages of HOPE from "US" (United Souls of Heaven and Earth)

New Vibrations
May 21, 2011

Dearest Beautiful Beings of Light,

You and your world have stepped into new vibrational patterns that you will not necessarily recognize at first; however, as you grow accustomed to these new vibrations you will assimilate them quite quickly as being *the way*—the way you will think, feel, act and express. The new vibrations you are experiencing are allowing you to move forward rapidly in your lives. New opportunities will open up instantly; others will shift and close or completely disappear. It will feel illusive for a while and leave you feeling like you are in a dream, until you embrace these transitions with the deep knowing that you are expanding not only your experiences but your beingness.

Your capacity to hold more light is increasing not just daily now, but minute by minute, and the energy that you feel moving through your physical systems is real and supporting this process of expansion. Even though it makes things feel a little surreal, we tell you that it is very real. The new vibrations are transmuting the densities at an accelerated rate that makes you feel like you are spinning and just want to get off the carnival ride. It can be exhilarating and exhausting all at the same time, and that is okay—you do get to choose how you experience this next bump up in your vibrational patterns.

You can resist and worry and try to keep the new at bay. Or you can welcome it, embrace it, take inspired action, and experience the Universal support for your transition into a vibrational energy that is more clear, pure and aligned with the truth of who you are as a Divine Being, as a human being who chose to be here at this time to hold the Light and anchor it on your Earth to illuminate the path for others.

As you embrace the new vibrations, it is important to not base anything on the past, as it is *all* new. Bringing in the past dilutes the purity of these new vibrations and the ease with which you can incorporate them into your lives and way of being. Create everything anew. Be open to new, fresh energy. In this new energy, your thoughts, inspirations, and guidance will support you to make decisions that align with this vibrational match.

Shifting, Shifting, Shifting

June 20, 2011

Dearest Beautiful Beings of Light,

You *are* shifting, Dear Ones. Even though it may not feel like it, as there has been a lull to allow you to release the energies that are no longer serving you, we want to assure you that you are shifting. Shifting the dense energies of doubt, worry, fear, restlessness, anxiety, physical pain, emotional pain, mental confusion and spiritual uncertainty so that you can more fully embody your truth.

If these energies have been coming up for you, know that you are not alone. It is happening for everyone on your planet, and when you are aware, they may seem more intense in the moment. For those of you who are aware, you may have noticed that they also shift much quicker. You do not have to be immersed in these energies and possibly overwhelmed by them like you have in the past. They are just clearing to allow the shift in vibration that you are ready for. We were going to say "the shift in vibration that *you want*," though it is more appropriate to point out that you *are* ready for these shifts in vibrations.

We spoke in our message last month about the new vibrations, and that is what you are shifting into. They are higher frequency, lighter, and much more accessible than they ever have been for you, because of your intent to hold Light, because of your intent to be in your truth and integrity, because of your willingness and dedication when it seems like nothing is happening (or too much is happening at once). You are not only willing participants in this shift in yourselves (and, we must point out, your planet), you are embracing these new energies with confidence and enthusiasm, which is accelerating their integration. And, of course, it is all about the integration, as without that process, it would be a futile endeavour, just going round and round.

We acknowledge you for the capacity you have shown in the integration of the new vibrations, because that is what is supporting the shift—the shift in your own physical manifestations, as well as the shift in your world. Shifting energy from doubt to trust, from worry to acceptance, from fear to love, from restlessness to patience, from anxiety to calmness, from physical pain to well-being, from emotional pain to joy, from mental confusion to clarity, and spiritual uncertainty to a deep inner knowing. This is what you are able to do as you receive many types of Universal support in your transition from density to Light. So we encourage you to embrace the energies, embrace one another, and know that all is well!

Messages of HOPE from "US" (United Souls of Heaven and Earth)

Supportive Energies
July 27, 2011

Dearest Beautiful Beings of Light,

We are here at this time of the Awakening, the Great Shift, to assure you that you are not alone. There are many energies, both physical and non-physical, to support your journey to becoming aware, to remembering who you are: the magnificent Light Being that always was and always will be, no matter what is happening in the moment (or did in the past or will in the future).

Supportive energies are coming to you in many ways, shapes, and forms. Some are tangible; some are intangible; all are relevant and powerful. You may have noticed many more synchronicities or alignments that happen quickly. This is not by chance. This is by orchestration—you and the Universe are operating more in co-creation that *ever* before. And we emphasize *ever* because it is all brand new. We have talked about this in previous channels, and when you allow the new—the new everything in your life, new way of thinking, new way of expressing, new way of being in relationship with others, new way of being in the world from a place of acceptance and love—you allow physical, as well as Universal, energies to support your new way of being.

One example would be this: If there was a difficult person in your life and you set the intent to shift the energy between you, many opportunities would be orchestrated for that to take place, such as crossing paths when maybe you really were uncomfortable with that, or just feeling an urge to say something supportive to them when it might not seem logical with what might have just occurred. You are receiving guidance from many realms, both Earthly and Heavenly, and when you let go of your "stuff", no matter how minor or major, it creates space for you to not only receive these supportive energies (you are getting them all the time), but to *feel* them physically as well as energetically. When you do, it creates a sense of relief, and it is a wonderful feeling that then allows you to open up to so much more—more support, more caring, more abundance, more peace, more joy and, most of all, more love.

Love is the ultimate supportive energy. It is the elixir of life that heals all. It is the potion that creates miracles. So as you tap into and become aware of the energies around you, give intent to be aware of the supportive energies within your own beingness, within others, within the Earth, and within the Universe, because they are all there for you to embrace at this time of the Great Shift. At this time, we are sending much love and supportive energy from the Cosmic realms to your Earth to activate what is already within you.

Messages of HOPE from "US" (United Souls of Heaven and Earth)

Merging Heaven on Earth
August 11, 2011

Dearest Beautiful Beings of Light,

The words "United Souls of Heaven and Earth" are very significant, because we would be from what you call Heaven, or something other than Earth; and you, your presence, is here now on Earth, and it is very timely that you connect to both worlds. It is about creating Heaven on Earth, and that the energies—whether they be our energies in the unseen dimensions, or your energies in the seen or the denser dimensions, the material dimension—now merge.

And that is our message to you this day. It is truly the merging of energies to create Heaven on Earth, not that you desire but that you know is possible; you know that it exists. You have had moments of having that experience of what you would term Heaven, or Utopia, or Shambala, or Nirvana. There are many terms that you have to express for what we will call Heaven for the purposes of this communication, because Heaven is all encompassing. Heaven is all of it—the unseen, the seen. It is supportive. It is all that ever was and ever will be, and all that is possible right now this moment.

It is not about having to analyze the past so that you know how to create the future. It is about being in the now that creates everything that you have ever wanted. As you keep your focus on whatever your knowing, perception, wishes, desires are of Heaven, that, Dear Ones, is what you are creating. And the message for you is that you can create this in the now without the struggle, without the pain, without the challenges. And as you create your own Heaven on Earth within your own physical being, you are so used to creating it in the external as in beautiful aesthetics, and we want to help you create that aesthetic from the inside so that it does not matter what your eyes are viewing in the external. You could be viewing something that you would not consider to be aesthetically pleasing but still have an aesthetically pleasing experience on the inside of you.

And that is what is happening. That is how you create your Heaven on Earth. Even though you want to create it in the external—and it is a necessary part of the equation—remember, Dear Ones, you get to create it on the inside first. And as you create that Heaven on Earth on the inside first, it shows up in your exterior. As you tune in to Heaven, or heavenly energies, you create it in your Earth, in your 3D time, and it actually gets anchored. So it becomes less of a vision or an intent and becomes a reality. We want to encourage you to hold that vision to create that for yourself, no matter what is going on in your physical reality.

Messages of HOPE from "US" (United Souls of Heaven and Earth)

Moving Forward
September 1, 2011

Dearest Beautiful Beings of Light,

August was a month of pulling back, laying back, experiencing the pleasures of life, and going inward. Much emotional debris was being cleared for you, if you were willing to let go and just feel and to trust that all was in Divine order—as it was. The Mercury retrograde that just ended is an opportunity for you to slow down, be more present in everything you are thinking and doing and allowing the momentum to build (like the tension on a slingshot) for the release and propelling forward. That is what you are now experiencing.

Be willing to take the next step that is presented to you, whatever that is. Much is being lined up by the Universe for the manifestation of your desires, and now it is up to you to take the action, however big or small. As we said in our last channel, there is much energetic support for your expansion as Light Beings; all you have to do is be willing and you will be shown.

The melding of Spirit with biology is in its completion stage, so you may be experiencing more intense physical symptoms, such as aches and pains, lethargy, foggy brain, mental confusion, digestive issues and emotional spikes. This is because your bodies are adapting to much higher vibrational energies than they've had available to them before.

Staying centred and balanced in your own knowing will serve you well over the next few months as your intuitive abilities are also expanding in conjunction with the anchoring of Light through your body. Trusting what is best for you will ultimately be best for all, even though it may not look like that in the moment. Honouring self, your Divine Self, is the fuel for your forward movement in all areas of your life. As you follow the nudges from within, events will line up and miracles will unfold before your very eyes.

Messages of HOPE from "US" (United Souls of Heaven and Earth)

Transformation at a Cellular Level

October 2, 2011

Dearest Beautiful Beings of Light,

You are in an intense period of transformation over the next six weeks leading up to the 11-11-11 gateway into the New World. This transformation is happening at a deep cellular level, and may be showing up as physical or emotional symptoms. You will find that you are happy and sad all at the same time, or in pain and comfort at the same time. It will feel like a dichotomy of experiences, and it is!

It is the duality, the sense of separation, leaving your systems and your emotional conditioning and programming, so you can truly feel your *oneness* with one another, as well as with the Universe. However, we want to focus on your oneness with one another and assure you that even though you may have stuff coming up with others in your life, know that it is the old programs being cleared at a cellular level. This is an integral part of moving forward into the next phase of your personal evolution as Creator beings, as Light Beings who are here at this time to create the New World, where you truly can live in harmony with each other.

Choice, Dear Ones, and your own awareness facilitate this transformation with either ease and grace or struggle and pain; that is why you are immersed in this dichotomy of energies and feelings. You get to experience how quickly denser energies can shift when you choose the higher vibrational energy or thought. As you do so, it triggers the coding in the cells of your body that have been dormant for a long time. You are now not only ready to activate, but are very capable of applying this awareness to any situation big or little, significant or insignificant (though nothing in your world is insignificant). Everything in your experience is there for a Divine purpose—we repeat, *everything*. Nothing is lesser or greater than in its purpose, no matter what it may seem.

Your cells now are capable of greater receiving and transmitting of higher vibrational information than has ever been possible in the physical body on your planet Earth. You are the conduits and transmitters of the Light language and love energy. Remember, we have said that the love that we speak of is an energy, not an emotion, and your cells are being activated to synchronize with that magnificent energy of love, not just from your heart, but from your cells. It is your choice how much of this beautiful, beneficial energy you allow to emanate from you and through you.

Messages of HOPE from "US" (United Souls of Heaven and Earth)

What's New Since 11-11-11?
November 30, 2011

Dearest Beautiful Beings of Light,

You are what's new since the 11-11-11 alignment of Cosmic Universal energy, Dear Ones! You may think you look the same, though your energy imprint is very different; you may even have had people comment that you look younger. And you are—on a cellular level. This alignment created much clearing on all levels—physical, emotional, mental and spiritual, and particularly on a heart level.

You may be experiencing relationships that were strained and are more loving now, and especially the relationship with yourself. That is the big transition you just went through. For those of you who are committed to your spiritual path: you may have experienced this before as you increase your vibration—it literally was a death and rebirth on an energetic level. You had the opportunity to do a life review while still in the same body and come out the other side with much greater awareness of who you are as a Divine Being more in touch with the Cosmic heart of all beings.

That is why it felt so intense for many of you. This was not just a little "bump up," as we have called it before. This was a catapult into the New Energy, the New World and, most importantly, the *New You*. The you that embraces all that is with passion and joy;

the you that is having a more grounded experience of what Light is; the you that feels the energy of love for everything and everyone especially for the beautiful Being of Light that is housed in your physical body.

The gateway you just passed through will allow you to feel less fear and experience more love than you have had the capability of doing ever before. The crystalline aspect of your physical body has been turned on to allow the amplification and reverberation of your beautiful Divine Essence with great awareness of your heart energy. The Light field and Light vibration that we spoke of in our channels is now fully activated for you to step into. All you have to do is be willing, even if you are not feeling it in the moment. Be willing to be the Light, be the Love—be *you*, the Being of Light that is anchoring this energy on your Earth and living it with every breath you take. So breathe in love and breathe out your beautiful Divine Light energy to the world. It *is* that simple!

Messages of HOPE from "US" (United Souls of Heaven and Earth)

Celebrating the New You in the New World

December 31, 2011

Dearest Beautiful Beings of Light,

Please take note of the word *new* in the title of our message to you this day of the crossing of a very significant threshold as you step in to the miraculous energy of your year of 2012. We emphasize the word *new* because that is what the energy will be for the next twelve incredible months of your human existence on Mother Earth. It is *all* new, and it is up to *you* how you perceive this newness—the newness in the external world and, most importantly, the newness of *you*.

Over these past few years of your spiritual awakening, you have been through much clearing, cleansing, re-organizing, transformation, transmutation, re-wiring, reconnecting, upgrading and re-creation of who you were only a very short time ago. And it is now time to be more conscious of that in a more empowered way. To stand up and own that you are a spiritually awakened being ready to share your life experiences with each other in a collaborative, honouring way to support the whole, thus creating a world you will choose to live in joyfully.

This year the stage has been set; the foundation has been laid to support the many changes necessary within your own personal being, as well as your world, to live in harmony. You will see major shift and change in all your infrastructures of government—institutions such as those of education, medicine, the environment, and many others as the players who will be instrumental in forging these changes have been in preparation and are feeling confident and supported to step out on centre stage. Each and every one of you will feel this within yourselves this year as you feel your passion and act on your role within the world scenario.

This will happen because you have become so much more clear on who you are as a Divine Being here on your Earth, to anchor the Light through your physical bodies and to be the expression of that Light in all aspects of your worldly existence. The *New You* will move so much more from love than from fear. Fear is of the old world, the old you. Love is building the New World and is the new energetic infrastructure that you as a human being have had rebuilt cell by cell in the energy systems of your physical body.

2012 will be the greatest expansion of the energy and vibration of love that humans on your planet have yet to experience, as well as the energy of collaboration and co-creation with many unseen energies here to support this shift to the new Age of Enlightenment for all, not for the special few. This en-Light-enment is the *new you*—Light embodied in physical form to bring about the miraculous changes you will see in 2012!

Messages of HOPE from "US" (United Souls of Heaven and Earth)

Embracing 2012

February 2, 2012

Dearest Beautiful Beings of Light,

As you are now a month into this incredible year of 2012, you will understand why we are using the word *embracing*, as there is already so much happening for you on so many different levels. As you embrace all of it—the ups, the downs, the ins, the outs, the intensity, the simplicity, the chaos, the stillness, the ebb, the flow—you will have a deeper and deeper knowing of who you are.

This year, many discoveries will be made on a personal level, as well as on a global level; it will take an acceptance of *what is* to access that deeper knowing, and the invaluable gifts that will be given to all as a result. This is the year to change all history. We have been telling you it is all new, and only you get to choose what is new is for you; it does not have to be based on past experience, past struggle or past pain—especially the pain. Many things will unfold this year to show you that you do not have to stay in the struggle and pain, and to show you the power you have to transcend these energies.

As you keep your hearts open, trust in yourself and others, and trust in your own inner guidance. The transformation of an uncomfortable situation will be instantaneous and create miracles in people's lives. We cannot emphasize enough the gifts you already have to raise the vibration of your world this instant. It begins with each and every one of you, individually, in your personal lives, in each moment, in each breath, in each thought, in each word—and then, of course, in each action to embrace the changes that are happening within your body, your mind, your emotions, and your spiritual awareness.

As this happens, you will experience a peace that is deep and profound, one that you will be able to share with others—like a contagious virus, only way more beneficial and empowering. You have chosen to be here on Earth at this time to anchor this peace, to exude your Light, and to share your joy, no matter what is happening in your personal life circumstances or global events. Embrace it all, knowing that it is all Divine—that you are Divine, and so is everyone else. As you consciously see that in yourself, you will automatically see it and feel it in others. And so will they.

We encourage you to embrace 2012 with an open heart and an open mind, knowing that you are always loved and supported from the realms of Love and Light. And now you get to do that on Earth.

Messages of HOPE from "US" (United Souls of Heaven and Earth)

Integrating Crystal Energy
February 26, 2012

Dearest Beautiful Beings of Light,

It is with great excitement that we send you words and information on the beautiful crystal energy that is being transmitted to you for activation from within your cells. Your cells have been going through an opening, clearing, and activation for a number of years now, and more particularly this past year. Crystal energy is highly tuned and very powerful, as you have seen through the use of your electronics. It only takes one tiny chip to send and receive a great amount of communication energy. So let your minds expand to perceive the implications of that: if every one of your trillions of cells could (and does) do the same thing, imagine the possibilities.

Crystal energy is pure and clear, just as your tangible examples are, like crystal chandeliers or crystal glasses. It is strong and delicate all at the same time and can amplify energy exponentially. It is intricate (like a snowflake) and simple (like a drop of water) all at once. Your body is the simplicity of the water that is being transformed into the intricacy of the snowflake with the energetic transformations that you are going through at a cellular level to amplify and transmit the pure Light energy within.

We know this sounds conceptual and esoteric. We hear you saying, "So how does this apply in the circumstances and challenges of my life?" You are a receiver and transmitter of energy, just like your electronics. You can receive and transmit energy that serves you, the ones you love, and your world—or you can receive and transmit energy that makes your life and your world more challenging and uncomfortable. This beautiful crystal energy will amplify either/or. It is up to you how you choose to use this energy through your thoughts and actions.

We used the word *integrating* in the title of this message as you are always receiving; now it is about you having a greater awareness for the integration process on a physical level so you can experience the benefits of what is happening *to* you, *for* you, and *by* you. Integrating means it is moving from intellectual awareness to a way of being that is automatic and free-flowing. It just *is*, and that is why we are here at this time—to help you to experience it. So be willing, be open to receive, make time in your day for awareness; the integration process will become more obvious to you in your everyday choices to feel the Light, be the Light, and share the Light with joy and love . . . so be it!

Messages of HOPE from "US" (United Souls of Heaven and Earth)

Vibrational Upgrade

April 3, 2012

Dearest Beautiful Beings of Light,

The month of March has seen exceptional advancement for the human species as it has been one of the most powerfully effective upgrades that you have yet to go through on a vibrational level. You may have experienced this as a lot of unsettledness and increased anxiety and fear of the unknown, as on some level you knew that is was moving you into a higher vibrational frequency that you were unfamiliar with. For some of you it created a pull back, a lull, and a lethargy that felt so deep you were not sure that you would be able to pull back out of it. We assure you that you are. It was a particularly necessary part of the next stage of your evolution.

As these higher vibrational energies integrate not only into your physical bodies, but into your Mother Earth, you will experience a settling at a core level within you, which will truly empower you to step out, take action, and express who you truly are on all levels—in your personal lives, in your careers, and on a global level. Pay attention to the shifts that will happen in the next few months from the microcosm of your individual lives and experiences, to the macrocosm of your global community, as well as in the Universe. Your awareness has been tweaked and amplified and will become much broader. Your awareness of physical energy, of vibration, of frequency, of what was felt though not seen, of dimensional energies and, most of all, Light signatures—*your* Light signatures (we will speak of this in future channels).

For upgrades to happen effectively, those of you in touch with energy have experienced what we call an *unplugging* for the upgrade to take place. Each of you get plugged back in a different time and frequency, so you are all having different experiences. Some of you have needed to rest and be very quiet; others have had to be physical and move the energy. Remember: you are all unique, and how you transmute energy is an individual process. Share your experiences with one another, but own your own; it is not better or worse than someone else's, just unique to you as your Light frequency is needed at this time to be anchored and expressed.

Things in your reality will look and feel different, and you will acclimate to this new vibration in your own time. Know that it is serving the whole of humanity as you accept, allow, and acknowledge your own Light and energy. Share it, speak of it, shine it, and take the actions that come from the feelings it generates as you now have a greater awareness.

Messages of HOPE from "US" (United Souls of Heaven and Earth)

Your Essence Is Blossoming
May 1, 2012

Dearest Beautiful Beings of Light,

Just as you are in the midst of the miracles of spring, seeing everything in your natural world blossoming, it is not only a metaphor, but a direct reflection of what is happening to you on a spiritual level. Your Divine Essence has been dormant, waiting for the perfect conditions to start to open up, to show its beauty and magnificence. And the right conditions are in place NOW! There is no more being invisible. The world is holding its breath while each and every one of you open the delicate petals of the new blossoms of Divine Energy that are being activated in you.

You may have noticed a deeper sense of knowing that has come upon you, though you are not yet sure what it is you know. Or that you are connecting with thoughts, images, and feelings that feel distinctly profound, though you are not quite able to express them. Are you aware that your intuition has been greatly enhanced, as well as your awareness of energy in general? We have told you in many channels that your abilities on all levels would be enhanced and that you would become more aware of the power you hold as creator beings.

And that blossoming of who you really are is now taking place in powerful ways for many of you who are able to accept the truth that you are Divine Beings on your Earth at this time. It is knowing at a deep level in your heart that you are here to make a difference, to be the Light for others who are still questioning and struggling to make sense of what is happening in their lives. Your coming out of dormancy and truly blossoming is the catalyst for many others to acknowledge the spiritual urge within themselves.

The world is truly ready for you to share your beauty, your grace, and your Light for all to see, experience, and resonate with. The vibrational upgrade you have embraced in the last few months will allow this to happen now with more ease and joy. You are emanating a higher frequency of love energy that will be felt by all in your presence, so go forth and emanate!

Messages of HOPE from "US" (United Souls of Heaven and Earth)

Clearing Discordant Energies

June 10, 2012

Dearest Beautiful Beings of Light,

You are receiving much support from the unseen realms to clear the discordant energies within your own physical being as well as the energetics of relationships, personally and globally. The first, and of utmost importance, is the relationship with yourself; then, as a natural result, with others in your life. As you move forward into the new, higher vibrational energy that has been anchored on your Earth, you will find that anything that feels the slightest bit discordant with who you are will feel amplified. That is for good reason: it is so it can no longer be ignored or excused.

As you become more and more consciously aware of energy, you will be more empowered to make conscious choices as to the energy you embody, as well as the energy you emanate. It is all part of the same package. If you are harbouring resentful, angry, or frustrated thoughts, that is the energy that you are emanating, even if you are trying to speak "nice" words. Congruency in thought, word, and action is the way of the New World; you may have noticed that when that is not happening within yourself or feeling it in others, it has become more and more uncomfortable. No longer will you be able to justify it.

You may have noticed an increase in unsettling dreams or thoughts passing through your mind, and that, Dear Ones, is your Divine Essence helping you to clear the discordant energies you have held in your body, your mind and your heart for so long. So just acknowledge these thoughts and feelings, and allow them to guide you to actions that will release the constrictions. The area of your body that has been the focus of the energy clearings of late is your heart. You may be having uncomfortable spasms in the chest area, amplified emotions, and irritability. Just know that this is part of the energetic clearing you are going through to be able to hold more of your Love and Light.

And there are those words we have spoken of many times: Love and Light. Say these words when you feel discordant with yourself or with others, and you will feel a shift of energy—physical as well as emotional—because, Dear Ones, it is all just energy, and you get to choose the energy that supports you.

Messages of HOPE from "US" (United Souls of Heaven and Earth)

Navigating Through the Intensities
July 10, 2012

Dearest Beautiful Beings of Light,

As you move closer and closer to the new awareness available to you, the new energy you are embodying on a more consistent basis now, the New World that *you* are creating, you are experiencing an intensity that is uncomfortable, though completely necessary—and, we must say, supporting you at the same time. It truly is like giving birth: there is intense pain, intense contractions, intense emotions, and for some even intense trauma and drama.

And know, Dear Ones, that it is all appropriate and beneficial to what is transpiring on an energetic, cellular level of your being-ness. Scream if need be, cry if you feel it—it is just the old, dense energies transmuting so you will whole-heartedly and full-bodily be able to embrace the treasure that you are creating. As you acknowledge the truth of what you are *really* feeling (not what you are *supposed* to feel as dedicated little "Light Beings"), the energy will alchemize much quicker and your lead will transmute into gold before your very eyes—or, should we say, right in your very heart, because that is where the alchemy is happening.

The vibration of your heart has amplified so you *feel* more now, and that is a little scary for some as you do not want to feel the negative emotions, though if you do not allow any feeling you will be shutting down the beautiful energy of joy as well. So give permission for your body and soul to help you transmute what feels dense, negative, or overwhelming. Your body and soul really do know what they are doing, so open up the space within you to feel the joy, feel the love, feel the support, feel the possibilities, feel the New Energy, feel the grander possibilities for yourself and your world.

It is all in perfect process right now, no matter how intense it might seem to you. The vibrational thermostat has been kicked up a notch and you *can* handle it. You have more strength, more power, more wisdom and more awareness now than you have ever had in your evolution from human beings to Light Beings, so own it and share it!

It is more important than ever to do things that bring you joy to keep your vibration high. Ignite that spark of who you are and consistently fuel it so that your flames of passion become the alchemical fire producing the gold.

Messages of HOPE from "US" (United Souls of Heaven and Earth)

The "Energy" of Joy

August 8, 2012

Dearest Beautiful Beings of Light,

You may wonder why we are calling our message the "*Energy* of Joy", as you probably consider joy to be an emotion. But if you stop to feel the truth of our words, you will understand the power of embracing this energy and embodying it as an expression of who you are!

You have many energies contained within your physical systems, some that are supportive and some that create challenges for you in your everyday life. What is changing for you, as we speak, is your ability to not only differentiate these energies, but to now be able to recognize, discern, and choose the energies you desire to work with to create your moment-to-moment experiences. You have always had this ability, though for the most part have allowed your experiences of energy by default, buying into someone else's experience through the media, cultural, or religious conditioning, as well as parental belief systems, peer consciousness, or the energies of mass consciousness.

Now it is time for you to take command of the energies available to you and choose the ones that support your journey to wholeness, your journey to peace and harmony, your journey to health and well-being, your journey to abundance, your journey to sustainability on your beautiful planet. And that comes about by being aware of the energy of joy, an energy that is very high vibrational that will, just by its sheer pure frequency, lift your thoughts to create a more empowered way of being. A way of being that exudes and expresses that joy on a more consistent, everyday basis, no matter what or who might be disturbing your energy of joy. You are the one in charge; you are the one who gets to cultivate and align with joy and thereby experience the myriad of emotions that are produced from conscious awareness of the Energy of JOY!

Choose JOY and you will be choosing a higher vibrational experience where much of the denser energies will not even be part of your experience any longer. JOY is the energy we are here to support you with as the Divine Beings that you are. You are here to anchor JOY on your Earth, and we are honoured to be the transmitters of this magnificent energy to you—the beautiful conduits. Take a breath and feel the energy of joy as it is being beamed to you and from you!

Messages of HOPE from "US" (United Souls of Heaven and Earth)

Energy Sensitivities
September 16, 2012

Dearest Beautiful Beings of Light,

As you embrace your *spiritual awakening*, you become more aware of the energy shifts—not only that of your beautiful planet and the Cosmos, but within your own being. You are changing at a cellular level and, as a result, may be noticing that you (and others around you) are being more "sensitive" to sounds, to smells, to light, to other's feelings and emotions, to your environments, and, as a result, not able to tolerate things that disturb you.

This is a natural process of raising the vibratory level in your body and will serve you well if you embrace it rather than resist it. It will even out eventually as things come into more balance in your world, though, in the meantime, it is important for you to stay centred in your core and to ground and clear your energy daily. There are many ways of accomplishing this, the main one being: BREATHE! We say that with emphasis as you have a tendency to constrict breathing when you feel shifts in energy. You may be experiencing it as anxiety because your body does not yet recognize the higher vibrational energy that you are receiving, so it is going into panic mode.

Your new sensitivities are your connection to the natural world as well as to the unseen world and are allowing you an enhanced perception of *all* that is—all that is working in your world, as well as all that is not working at the moment. So as you honour what your body is telling you it resonates with (or does not), you are creating a stronger and more vital energy field. A strong energy field creates a healthy body and a balanced mind and emotions. And, most importantly, a strong energy field emanates that beautiful Light from within, your Divine Essence being housed in comfort, and able to exude and be expressed in ways that are supportive and beneficial to you and all those you interact with.

This day aligns with new moon energy and an opportunity to consciously embrace the new energies you are embodying as the energy shifters of your world. We assure you that you have more power than you are yet aware of, and that you truly are making a difference. We honour you as the Light Beings that you are!

Messages of HOPE from "US" (United Souls of Heaven and Earth)

Heightened Awareness
October 9, 2012

Dearest Beautiful Beings of Light,

In our last communication, we spoke of how you and your world are evolving into higher frequencies, and how there is a corresponding shift in your sensitivities, your awareness of subtle, and not-so-subtle, energies around you. Some of the energies that you are becoming more aware of or are sensing are multi-dimensional in nature—energies that have always been accessible to you, though now you are choosing at some level to be more aware of them. As we said before, this is all part of the spiritual awakening that is happening on a cellular level for human beings.

You have an innate knowing that is surfacing—being activated, actually—about dimensional energy. These are frequencies, vibrations, resonances, holograms and many more concepts that at one time might have been viewed as primarily scientific, but then became New Age terminology. Now these concepts are becoming everyday household terms used in conversations as the knowing of what these words really mean comes to your cognitive awareness. This awareness not only of understanding concepts and meanings, but the sensing of the experience of these terms, has taken a quantum leap as you move through 2012. It is the way of being now, not just the academic espousing of knowledge.

For some of you, it is becoming second nature to sense things you never have before, such as: others' thoughts or feelings; things going on in your global world events or the world of nature that you then hear about on the news; hearing sounds that you have not noticed before; feeling energy deep inside your body; having moments of no time, no space (where past, present, and future are not what they seem—they overlap); sensing unseen worlds, as you are now accepting that there is so much more than what you can see with the human eye—though that is being amplified as well as many of you are experiencing things like a wider range and vibrancy of colour or images.

As you embrace and give conscious intent for heightened awareness, it is amplified for you. It will serve you greatly in the times to come; these senses will be invaluable in the decisions you will make in navigating through the shifts and changes you and your Earth are going through as you birth the New Age of peace, love, joy and harmony. This New World is being created through the heightened awareness that is expressed through of each and every one of you in whatever endeavours you choose to engage on a daily basis. We support you in sensing all the power you already have within to shift energy.

Messages of HOPE from "US" (United Souls of Heaven and Earth)

Dimensional Doorways
November 6, 2012

Dearest Beautiful Beings of Light,

We are continuing with our transmission of information about dimensional energy, particularly dimensional doorways. There are many of you who are seers that are very aware of the concept of dimensional doorways and who have also had the physical experience of passing through those doorways. Now, as is happening with all aspects of your human evolution, each and every one of you is having the experience of sensing dimensional doorways, and even though you do not know exactly what is happening on a practical level, you have a deep knowing of how profound this is.

You experience forgetting everyday things that felt important, and then realize you are able to re-adjust circumstances and that everything is just fine. This will continue to happen as you move more into the new energy of these next few years as the old energy dissipates. Not just the old structures of your world—governmental, educational, medical, financial—but, most importantly, the mental structures of your humanness.

The old views, beliefs, conditioning, and patterns are being erased for a clean slate to create new ways of being in higher vibrational energy. Have you noticed that you are letting more of the little things go, not making such a big deal of them, or not wanting to get drawn into other people's dramas? That is because in the other dimensions drama is not part of the energy, and you are being prepared to exist in the higher dimensional energies in an interconnectedness that few have experienced to this point.

Moving through dimensional doorways is giving you the sense of no time and no space, and that is exactly what it is—even though to your logical mind it is confusing and unsettling. Trust that it supports the emergence of the new coalesced expression of who you are that has complete access to higher knowing, therefore leaving behind what no longer serves your way of being—particularly your way of *thinking*.

As you trust the process, even if you don't understand it, you will find a deeper peace from within as well as a greater sense of freedom from the constrictions of the world as it has been. You can create the world as you want it to be, with much dimensional support from the other realms of existence.

Messages of HOPE from "US" (United Souls of Heaven and Earth)

Alignment of Energies
December 9, 2012

Dearest Beautiful Beings of Light,

The theme of our transmissions of late has been about energy, and we will continue to support you in understanding the alignment of energies that is happening on Cosmic and physical levels for each of you on Earth. This time has been long predicted and prophesied by indigenous cultures that were much more connected to the Earth, as well as to the Universe, than humankind is today—though, because of the power of these alignments, that is about to change.

As your Earth continues her journey through the centre of the Galaxy, it creates many portals or vortexes that open to higher vibrational emanations to Earth and, of course, to human beings as you are the conductors of this Light energy. The many numerological alignments that have preceded this particular upcoming alignment of 12-12-12 have been in preparation for the shift in consciousness that will happen at a much more accelerated rate, more instantaneous than it has been to this point. All it takes is being willing to literally see the Light in yourselves, first and foremost, then in others, and then in everything, even if you don't intellectually understand it yet.

As the broad spectrum of energies—from the darkest dark to the lightest light—blend and harmonize, you may feel that you do not have your bearings, because what you knew to be true about yourself and your world are changing at lightning speed. And it is very necessary for you to feel the power you have within for creating the New World. All the aspects of your own personal energies are aligning in conjunction with the alignment of the Earth and the Universe, so it feels "out of this world"—and it is! Your bodies are no longer able to hold onto the density; it is being flushed, erased, eradicated, transmuted and transformed, thus the physical discomfort many of you are experiencing. This too shall pass as you focus your energy in the now and the resonance of the possibilities of the *New You* and the new Earth.

The energies of joy and love are the two most powerful alignments in the Universe, and they are yours for the choosing. We support you in embodying these alignments with ease and grace.

Messages of HOPE from "US" (United Souls of Heaven and Earth)

Hold Your Sacred Space... 12-12-12 Activation at 12:12 p.m.

December 12, 2012

Dearest Beautiful Beings of Light,

We are the United Souls of Heaven and Earth, and it brings us great delight to be in the presence of such magnificent Light Beings. Those of you who have been with "US", and with our host before, have heard those words many times and we want to tell you that you are actually "getting it." As we say these words, we feel their integration with the energy and the activations at much deeper levels than ever have been in any of our channels—whether they be live, or over the phone. As we say the words, the energy actually *is* integrating.

This part of our message for you, on this day of the 12-12-12 alignment, is as follows:

Many of you are out there seeking, searching, wondering, questioning, at crossroads in your existence in your personal lives, in your careers, in your spiritual lives. We strongly want to impart to you the message and the energy that you are *there*, and that it is happening. Do not doubt, Dear Ones. Do not question, no matter what seems to be showing up in your external world, or even in your personal circumstances. There are still logistics to work out in your energetic systems, as well as your personal life systems, to know, and be assured, that it *is* done! All of the work that you have done to this point, in not only your personal life, but in human existence, has all been coming together for this exact point in time.

This 12-12-12 alignment, as our host alluded to in her opening talk with you, is the alignment of your Mastery. It is an energy that many of the Ascended Masters, many of your spiritual teachers, have been emanating to you, have been sending teachings to you—not just for centuries, but for eons. And now, Dear Ones, guess what is happening? It is coming *through* you; we have said this many, many times. This alignment of this day is the height of that energy of the Mastery of who you truly are as a Divine Being, as a Spiritual Being, as a Light Being—but also as a human being, because it is all melding into one now. There is no separation, and the energies of these alignments of the 12-12-12 and December 21st both add up to 11.

As you embrace the energy of that, of the Mastery of what is happening to you and through you right now in your life (on a personal level as well as on a Cosmic level), you will realize there actually is no separation. It is the melding of all into O*neness*, all into *wholeness*, all into *unity*, all into *harmony*. And as you make room and space in your awareness, and in your time/space continuum for that to happen, it will happen at a much quicker rate.

One of the things that has been going on very intensely in these past few weeks, few months, and few years, is deep internal cleansing and clearing. We know again, Dear Ones, that is a powerful piece of your moving into the Light, of you embodying the Light, of your being the Divine Essence that you came here to be, to anchor that on your Earth. As you are going through all of these clearings and awareness, give thanks, be grateful, and understand that something much bigger than what you could ever understand is happening to you and through you. The energy that you have allowed yourself to connect to in different ways is this Cosmic Universal Energy that is coming together as your Mother Earth moves into alignment.

Part of what is happening is that Mother Earth is moving into her own alignment. Because of your connection with Her body and your bodies, *your* body has to adjust to these energies to also move into alignment of the higher frequencies, the higher vibrational energy. We have spoken of this many times; this 12-12-12 alignment *is* the boost. It is a boost for each and every one of you, not just those who have chosen to be on call or in meditation this day; it is happening for everyone. There are those of you who have the awareness of this alignment, of having awareness that the consciousness is being expanded, who have the awareness that your vibration is being raised. Having the awareness that you are tuning in at a higher frequency energy will have that integrated and embodied with greater ease.

And that, Dear Ones, is what is happening for you—if you allow it. When you step off into doubt, worry, fear, or old patterns which are coming up in great force (because, of course, as you set an intention for something greater, for something more expanded, everything that is not of that vibration will show itself to be cleared), it comes up in the contrast. As you acknowledge what is coming up, you help dissipate the energy. It is coming up for you, Dear Ones: at night in your dreams; in your everyday mind chatter; in your interactions with others who do not understand what is happening to them. And it is for each and every one of you to hold your sacred space.

That is our message to you this day, on this 12-12-12 alignment: hold your sacred space, no matter what is happening in your external world. No matter what is happening in your mental world, acknowledge it and *choose* to hold your sacred space, because that is the vibrational energy; that is what will support you; that is how you connect to your Source; that is how you allow your Divine Essence to be expressed. That is the next phase for each and every one of you now: as you hold your sacred space, your Divine Essence will have a container for its expansion, a container for its expression.

We have said this in many channels before: it is time, Dear Ones! It is time for you to give voice, to give action to that expression of who you truly are, in whatever form that is aligning with *you*. And there are so many of you on this call that have stepped into that in writing your books, in creating your art, in creating your music, in expressing what you know to be true—not only for yourselves, but for your world! And we want to add an extra piece that is not only for your world: Dear Ones, it is for the Universe, because *all* is connected.

We have said many times that it is not just "US" in the other realms giving energy, or information, or activations to you; it is because of your choices that everything is shifting, and that the awakening is happening. Because you hold your sacred space, are being true to yourself, are allowing your Divine Essence to come forth, the shift is happening quickly. As you do that, it is transforming and shifting for "US" as well, because even though we are in another frequency, another bandwidth, another dimension than you are, there is so little separation now that the effect you have on everything is much more powerful, is much more profound, and also much more expansive.

As you truly own that place within you, knowing that you are aligning with your own sacred space, *that* is how you are changing everything. There are many Cosmic alignments happening to support that. You are, Dear Ones, moving out of the dark ages, but some will choose to stay there for a while. And there may be even some of those moments for you. Our Host ("US" is referring to Judith here) had a few of those this week, moments when she felt like she was still in a sort of 'dark ages' in her thinking, while realizing it was just passing through, it was just leaving, it was just the transformation that was happening to truly step into the Light, to truly be that embodiment.

As these alignments happen, they support that process for each and every one of you. And as you make the choice to be in your own sacred space—each and every moment, not just sometimes—this is the piece that is changing; this is the piece that you are receiving support for, which will be much easier from this day forward. We do not normally say things quite so specifically, but we want you to know, and to hold that in your vibration, that from this day forward, the expression of who you are will absolutely get easier. As you own that truth, Dear Ones, you will have a greater influence on the ALL.

That is one of the pieces that unsettles you: the awareness that you can have an effect on the ALL. Not just human influence, not just global influence, but Universal influence. Part of the message we have been imparting to you over the last few channels is about *energy*, about how powerful you as conduits of this energy are in the transitions happening on ALL levels. We want to express that again: The changes that are happening on ALL levels. The ALL is the Oneness. It is happening through *you*, through each and every one of you in what you may feel are your insignificant lives, which are absolutely the opposite of that. Each and every life on this Earth, each and every person on your Earth, is much more significant than anyone has ever told you.

We are telling you right now, on this day, with this alignment, the significance, the magnificence, the brilliance, all of the wonderful terms we would come up with to show you to allow you to have the physical experience of the power that you have within you. Because this is what is happening on this day, on this alignment, as you hit the top of the energy wave that will lead you into years and decades and centuries of an enlightenment energy that has already been orchestrated and is in place for those of you who hold your sacred space.

We leave you now with great joy, with honour. We want to express the word *honour* for the journey that you have taken to bring not only yourselves, but humanity, Mother Earth, and the Universe in alignment.

Messages of HOPE from "US" (United Souls of Heaven and Earth)

Breathe Your Light...
12-21-12 Activation

December 21, 2012

Dearest Beautiful Beings of Light,

We are the United Souls of Heaven and of Earth, and it brings us great delight to be in the presence of such magnificent Light Beings. As we have said to you in our two previous channels, that term is not as necessary for us to repeat as we had to for these previous months, because you *have* evolved and are now at the stage where you are getting it—not on an intellectual level, but on the cellular level. From our perspective, it makes our—we were going to say *work*, and we are going to change that—our *mission* easier, because you are more in sync with "US" and our vibration. That is good news, Dear Ones, because you have been preparing for this for a very, very long time. Not just years, not just decades, not just centuries, but many cycles. As our Host said ("US" is referring to Judith), many cycles of human evolution have gone into the making of this point in time, at this moment, this day.

We want you to really *feel* that—the power of this moment—because it is that power of who you are as the Light Being that has made this moment possible. If it were not for each and every one of you moving through your "stuff,"—seeking a higher knowing, embracing all there is to know on all of the dimensions—this moment may have looked very different in your human evolution. But because there are so many of you out there at this time that own who you are, who *are* owning who you are, that has made it possible to have peace on your Earth at this time. And yes, it may still not look like that on the exterior—but know, Dear Ones, that it truly is done! That the energy fields, the resonance, the vibration has been laid on your Earth up to . . . working up to this date, but as of this date, it is like the clock has struck midnight for you, and it is like everything is truly magical in its alignment with the Cosmos.

Be ready for many miracles to happen in your life. And even as we use that word *miracles*, there is a shift happening even around that word, because it is not going to be *miraculous*; it is going to be *norma*l. It is normal at this point in your evolution for many wondrous things to happen, for synchronicities to happen just because you *are* who you are! That is our message to you on this day of December 21st, 2012—there, again, the energy of 11, of your Mastery, of truly stepping into your power and being, and exuding who you are. It's because of owning who you are that all of this has happened in your world, and that will continue to build.

As the energy and the frequencies are being resonated from *you*, Dear Ones—and we want to say that one again—as the energy and the frequencies are being resonated from *you*, Dear Ones, the shifts will happen quicker, and quicker, and quicker, and quicker. We have said this in many of our channels: it is still just about you aligning with your truth. Being who you already are as a Divine Being, as a Light Being. As the portals open on this date, there are many groups and gatherings all around your globe that are happening in succession on this date; many of your seers knew this time to be significant because of the activations that are happening in your land, in your Mother Earth, in Her structures, in Her sacred places, in Her pyramids, in the stones, in the crystals.

So, Dear Ones, our message to you always has been, always will be (no matter how many times you hear our words, it will slightly alter to give you a bigger perspective) that you *are* the Sacred Ones. You *are* the Divine Ones. You are *are* Light Beings. It is through you, Dear Ones, that this is happening. And yes, there are great Cosmic alignments happening with the Sun, the Earth, the stars, the planets, and the pyramids, and the sacred spots and the stones, but it is happening because of *you!* Because you, Dear Ones, got your planet to this point. This point in time could have looked very, very different, but because of you (and that is our message, and we are going to say it over, and over, and over to you this day), this moment in time is possible.

As you are letting that energy in—knowing the truth of our words, of the transmission of the energy to you—take a big and deep breath, Dear Ones, because it is that cellular activation that is allowing the shift to happen at quantum speed. It is a shift at your cellular level that is allowing the shift at quantum speed. It is because of your permission. It is because of your willingness. It is because of you stepping up to the plate. It is because, Dear Ones, each and every one of you are allowing your truth to emerge. You are allowing your Mastery to emerge. You are embodying your Mastery. You are embodying your Light. You are embodying your Divinity.

As you go through this day in particular, holding that in your consciousness, you are not doing it, Dear Ones, just for you, not just for yourself. You are doing it for all of mankind. You are doing it for all of the dimensions. Dear Ones, you are doing it for all of the Universe! So it is this interconnectedness that is happening on this is day on these alignments that will allow you to see from not just your inner perspective, but truly you will start to see it in the external perspective now of the shifts that *have* happened. And as you focus on all the great shifts that have happened, and let go of what has not (in your perspective) lined up yet, the energy that you embody will be amplified because of it.

This is a time of great amplification for each and every one of you. As you are in that vibration of the truth of who you are in that knowing of your Light Beingness, that is the entrainment that happens with all the others who may not have had your opportunities to see the Light, who may not have had the push from within, have not recognized that push from within. But because you have done it, it will happen so quickly it will truly make your head spin. As you see in your mind's eye your Light from within and truly breathe it, Dear Ones, that is all you have to do—just breathe your Light. Just breathe your Light. Just breathe your Light. That is how simple it can be. That is how graceful it can be: just breathe your Light.

As you take those words and energy into your holiday season—and when you feel the chaos, or the frenzy, or all of the other old stuff that is leaving—remember those words, those three little words that will assist you to come back to your core. As a result, guess what happens, Dear Ones? You allow others then to come back to their core. Those three little words—*breathe your Light*—are all that it takes, all that it takes on this day of the alignment, all that it will take on tomorrow's day of alignment, on the next day of alignment, on the next day, and in all of your beautiful holiday celebrations; that is what it is about. It is the *Light*. You are moving from a time of darkness, a time of density, a time of much turmoil—not just in your world, but in the Cosmos—that is now dissipating. Each and every one of you is having an experience of more and more; even our Host, as she was going through her week and not feeling physically on top of her game, her old patterns were coming up with her thinking that she was not doing enough, that she was not holding the Light, that she was not creating sacred space. We want to assure her and anyone else who has been having those thoughts these past few weeks that you truly *were*, and you *are*, so breathe Light. That is all it takes, Dear Ones: just breathe your Light.

As you have thoughts that are clearing, we want to assure you they are not in your cells any longer. They *are* clearing. So if you choose to hang onto them, know that is your choice. There has been much Cosmic support for the cleansing, the clearing, the rewiring, the transformation, the transcendence—any word we can think up— to help impart to you what has truly happened these last few years, on a very physical level, for each and every one of you . . . .that it has happened on a physical level.

It is that physical level that is now transcending into the Light. You are going to have more and more experience of Light in your bodies: Light behind your eyes; Light in your cells; Light in your hands; Light emanating from you; Light emanating from others.

We have said this a couple of years ago, and many of you are now experiencing that on a greater level. Hold on to your socks, Dear Ones, because that was only a teensy, teensy, teensy-weensy particle of what you will now experience after this day of alignment. That Light is the energy of your Beingness. Light is the energy that will come through your eyes. Light is the energy that will come through your beautiful smile. Light is the energy that people will feel from you when they stand in your presence. Light is the energy, almost like lightning, that will go through people when you touch them. The energy of Light will become so much more in awareness, because of the path that each and every one of you has chosen to this point.

As of this day of the ending of one cycle and the opening another, you have stepped through a portal—a very grand portal of energy, Dear Ones, that is allowing you to embody it on a greater, and greater, and greater, and greater, and greater level. It is just thought now. So, as we said earlier, when you have thoughts of less-than-ness, of worry, of fear, acknowledge it and then just breathe your Light. Breathe your Light. Breathe your Light, because there still will be energies that are passing through. Many of them will not even be your own, Dear Ones, as many of them are still from the mass consciousness. Know that this is okay! As we are working with your energy at this time, we are helping you shift, to allow the energy just to move through. It does not need to get stuck in your bodies any longer. You are a clear and pure vessel and, as you accept that for yourself, the energy can move much more freely.

As you breathe your Light, see it move through your body. See it move to Mother Earth. See it move to the Cosmos. See it emanate from you. We are working with each and every one of your energy fields at this time because you have been so dedicated to be with "US", to be with our Host in our gatherings, that you are receiving an extra boost of amplification. We were going to say *clearing* but that is not actually what we are doing this day. In the last channel we did lots of clearing. With this transmission, we are actually doing amplification so the energy can move through you. All of that beautiful Light energy can just move through you, exude through you, expand from you to resonate through you to just breathe your Light.

We leave you now, Dear Ones, with the transmission, the words, the energy, and with our great love and honour for your journey.

Messages of HOPE from "US" (United Souls of Heaven and Earth)

Moving Into the Year 2013... What Now?

December 31, 2012

Dearest Beautiful Beings of Light,

We in the other dimensions are very aware of the question that your humanness is asking now that you have passed over the threshold of December 21, 2012, and through the Cosmic portals and alignments that just happened to your Earth. You are all having varied experiences, depending on many factors of where you are on your spiritual journey, in your personal evolution and your connectedness with Spirit.

There are those of you out there who are transmuters of energy, so are experiencing much dense, chaotic, old energy leaving your mind, your body, and your experiences as they are presenting themselves to be acknowledged and released. Know, Dear Ones, that it is your Light that is illuminating these energies for clearing, not just the Cosmic emanations. You are clearing for the masses, as well as for Mother Earth. Whenever there is a shift of such magnitude that occurred this past few weeks there is always the intensifying of the contrast as well. So acknowledge it and bless it, whether it be in yourselves, in others, or in events; know that it is shifting at a Universal level, not just the human level, as you are an intricate component of the Universal makeup.

As tomorrow is the first day of the energy that the year 2013 is gifting to you, know that you get to choose what to do with it. Yes, it is of higher vibration, and yes, it is powerful, so align your power with it.

You ask, "What does *that* mean?"
Your power is *your* truth—what is *your* truth?
Your power is *your* passion—what is *your* passion?
Your power is *your* joy—what brings *you* joy?
Your power is *your* unlimitedness—what are *your* possibilities?
Your power is *your* personal creation—what are *you* creating in this new energy?

Focus your energy and intentions on creating what has not seemed possible before, as the energetic support has been laid in the Light fields that surround you to allow for instant manifestation. You do not need to know all the whys and hows; just acknowledge the power within you (and others) to create the new and magical combination of circumstances and awareness that will show you the tangible application of the higher frequencies now available to you. As the magnificent Light Beings that you *know* you are, go forth and create all that you have ever wished for and desired for your world, and do it with the energy of joy and love. It will take you far.

Messages of HOPE from "US" (United Souls of Heaven and Earth)

Benefiting from The New Energies
January 24, 2013

Dearest Beautiful Beings of Light,

When we use the word *benefiting*, it is our desire to instill in you the deep knowing, as well as the vibrational alignment, that you *are* most definitely benefiting from the shift your Mother Earth has just made in the Cosmos into higher dimensional vibrations. We acknowledge that even though it may be a little disorienting to some and amplified for others, you are truly benefiting on levels that will soon be very noticeable. Allow yourselves to feel what would be most beneficial to you in your life, as well as beneficial to others, and then know that just by thinking the thought, and feeling the feeling, you have aligned with the new energies because they are the power behind the creation of a world that works for all.

How can that be? It is by accepting that there are many ways to attain the same desired result, and it is the uniqueness that each human brings to the mix that allows the alchemical process of changing from one thing to another, from changing from fear to love, from discordance to peace, from illness to health, from lack to abundance, from despair to joy. We assure you that these shifts *are* happening.

Look for the evidence; notice the little (and not so little things) happening in your everyday life. Give your attention and energy to those things that line up easily, rather than fretting about those that don't. Give your focus to where your body is getting stronger and healthier rather than the aches and pains. Give your thoughts and words of communication to what is working, rather than what is not. Even using the words *I am benefiting from* will shift the energy from suffering to beneficence.

The energy of beneficence is now amplified in your Light field. The energetic harmonics of using the beautiful word beneficence will go a long way in creating what you truly desire for yourselves and your world to live in harmony.

Messages of HOPE from "US" (United Souls of Heaven and Earth)

Being Cocooned

February 20, 2013

Dearest Beautiful Beings of Light,

There are *so* many alchemical processes going on at once in your physical bodies at this time that many are feeling like they are needing to cocoon, to enclosed themselves in a sacred, quiet, safe space undisturbed by the outer discordances of your world. And we want to assure you that is okay. As much as possible, create that space for yourself as it will assist the transmutation that is taking place at a cellular level. This is happening for all those on your Earth, though it is much more accelerated and amplified for those of you who are conscious of what is happening and willing to go with it rather than resisting it.

You are morphing, shifting, transforming, breaking down, releasing, renewing, regenerating, and re-creating your physical bodies, and it is an uncomfortable and unsettling process because there is no precedent, and therefore nothing to fall back on for answers other than your own internal guidance. When you close your eyes, and truly go inside and tune in to your body, you will feel the miraculousness that is happening and will know how to support yourself through this transition. You will know what to do to create comfort for yourself, because, as you tune in, you will feel that peace from within that is the essence of who you really are as a Light Being.

There is a Universal cocooning going on as well, an enfolding or encapsulating energy that is supporting you. You may have noticed a feeling of not wanting to be out in the world or wanting to interact with others right now; that is the Cosmic energy swathing your body and your mind to just rest and allow the release of the denseness you have held for eons—the denseness of physical matter, the denseness of thought, and most significantly the denseness of emotion. Old emotional energy is being cleared from your cellular memory, so as a result, it has had to come to the surface to be released. Again, we encourage you to just allow and not judge what you are feeling. Find healthy ways to shift it, such as extreme self-care, loving support from others, and sharing your experiences as it reassures each of you that you are not slipping backwards or going downhill as we know how important it is to each of you to feel like you are making a difference, and expanding your consciousness and raising your vibration, not constricting it.

This process does not mean you are going backwards in any way shape or form, or constricting your beauty and your Light. It means you are willing to be the conduit for the shift of the mass consciousness from denseness to light, from fear to love, and from suffering to joy; that is what is happening on an energetic level in the cells of your body right now, and we assure you there is much seen and unseen support for this alchemical process. There are many mentors in your physical realm that have been prepared for this moment in time. Seek them out; you will feel the vibrational match as you trust your inner guidance and your truth.

Messages of HOPE from "US" (United Souls of Heaven and Earth)

New Energy Concepts Being Integrated

March 26, 2013

Dearest Beautiful Beings of Light,

The words and energy we have shared in our recent transmissions have been specifically directed to your physical bodies as they are going through much transmutation and transcendence at this time. Today we are focusing on your brain and your mind as, of course, they are an integral part of you not only being human, but also your Light Being-ness.

There are many old-energy concepts that are being purged from your energy systems and, particularly, your mind. The way you will understand and work with energy from here on in will be very different than you have been used to. Energy is malleable and can be extremely powerful, as you have learned through misuse of many of your power sources. The energy we are referring to is that which is contained within you, in your body and in your mind. Your mind is a powerful tool of creation; what has been happening of late is the shutting down of your brain for the necessary upgrades, rewiring and downloading of the New-Energy concepts that you are finally ready for. We are not necessarily referring to new belief systems; however, those are part of the process.

through Judith Onley

You have been going through many processes, both consciously implemented by you and those you are unaware of, orchestrated by the Cosmos, releasing old energy that has kept you limited, constricted, and feeling frustrated as you know that you are *so* much more than what you have been told or conditioned to believe. The New-Energy concepts have been beyond your realm of knowing up to this point; that has begun to change at lightning speed, leaving you wondering, *What is it that I really believe, know, and feel?*

As you answer those questions for yourself, you will not only be quite surprised at your answers, but empowered and extremely inspired into action of implementation on many different levels.

These past few months have been a necessary process of the integration of the New Energy through the body; now you will be much more aware of the upgrading going on in your brain that will allow the expression of these New-Energy concepts through your mind and expression in your everyday life. We want to emphasize the words *everyday life* because, Dear Ones, that is really where the power of this New Energy begins, and radiates, in each moment, in each breath, in each thought, in each word and each action that each of you will take, consciously applying the higher vibrational energy available to you now.

Messages of HOPE from "US" (United Souls of Heaven and Earth)

Going with the Flow with Ease

April 22, 2013

Dearest Beautiful Beings of Light,

Many shifts of energy and changes in circumstances are about to begin in many of your lives as a result of these past few months of clearing, purging, rewiring, renewing, integration and rebooting taking place on all levels of your physical existence within your bodies. Though it may have been an uncomfortable process for some (because of the not-knowing that you have been experiencing), it was necessary to get you out of your minds, of having to figure it all out.

What has been happening has been beyond your comprehension at this point and will now become clearer for you. There has been much orchestration going on in the Cosmos, in the other dimensions, to bring energies, circumstances, people and possibilities together for your support and movement forward in the new energies that now exist on your Earth for your expansion and expression as Light Beings.

Going with the flow of what comes into your awareness, whether you deem it good or bad (as that is just a human judgement), will allow you to know, see, and feel things that you would never thought possible. Going with the flow of what is being presented to you, rather than resisting it, will take you to the next vantage point where you will have the understanding of why certain things are taking place in your life.

The energy flow in your bodies, as well as in your Earth, is accelerating; resisting the changes will cause struggle and challenge. Accepting, going with the flow and choosing a higher perspective will create ease within your body, ease within your mind, and, most importantly, ease within your heart.

The shifts and change are facilitating a great expansion of heart energy, and when you are tuned into your heart energy, you will automatically feel the ease, feel the flow. It all goes hand in hand, leading you forward out of the struggle. All you have to do is be willing. You do not need to know the how, or the details of what is unfolding. It will be presented as you make the next choice—and, of course, choosing from your heart raises the vibration not only of your energy field, but that of your Earth. That is how you influence global change for the highest good of all.

Go with the flow of what your heart feels, create ease in your life, and you influence many.

Messages of HOPE from "US" (United Souls of Heaven and Earth)

Opening Up to More
May 20, 2013

Dearest Beautiful Beings of Light,

There is an energetic expansion happening on so many levels now; it has created an opposite and extreme reaction by many, actually closing down rather than opening up and expanding who you are. Over the past few months it has been important to be more inward, to sense your core being, to incubate, to insulate, to self-discover, to observe and to explore the inner realms.

During that process there has been much clearing, recalibration, and rebalancing happening on a cellular level; now it is time to open up to more manifestation in the physical. Because there has been so much expansion energetically, you have needed to just be in it, and now you are able to apply it and use it to express in the outer world more definitively and constructively. Your minds are able to hold more information at a higher vibrational level, and your bodies have been cleared of much density to hold more Light. Not only will you feel it in others (and yourself, of course), but you will actually be able to see it with your physical eyes.

We have spoken before of Light energy; now you have the capacity to understand it on a greater cognitive level as well as embody it on a physical level. Many of you walking a spiritual path have been put through your paces lately, facing old energy that is no longer serving you. And you are willingly moving out of it. As a result, this is opening the flow of more Cosmic energy to your Earth through you as the conduits. When this is done with intent, it creates an opening in your own personal energy field for the flow of circumstances and opportunities to come to you that have not been a vibrational match up to this point.

As you understand more about vibration and frequency, you will be able to allow the flow of energy in much greater capacities—not just through your bodies and minds, but through your hearts. So many have felt like they have needed to protect their hearts; now, all of a sudden, you will know that is no longer necessary. You will feel a fullness in your heart that will truly *runneth over*, and as this happens you will be open to receiving more Light, more love, and more support on all realms of existence—not just the physical. There is an alignment that has happened in all dimensions because of your willingness to walk the human journey and anchor the Light on your Earth. You will now see the effects of this in your personal lives as well as on a global level.

Opening to more means more of everything—not just what you desire to attain as material manifestation, though that is one of the byproducts. It involves opening to more of who you are as a powerful Being of Light that is here at this time to facilitate the transition of your world from density to Light, from fear to joy, and to embrace all the outwardly creations that Being-ness will initiate and draw into your everyday existence. Be ready and open, as there is so much more for you to have and *be!*

Messages of HOPE from "US" (United Souls of Heaven and Earth)

Living in the New Energy
June 30, 2013

Dearest Beautiful Beings of Light,

You are at the halfway mark of 2013, and many of you are now ready to live fully in the new energy that is available to you and your Earth. You have come through much clearing and recalibration in the past six months, and feel like you can literally see the Light and feel the Light in yourself and in others. For that to be anchored at a deep, core level, you have seen the density or darkness come up as well.

The contrast is what empowers you, if you acknowledge it and are willing to do whatever is necessary to shift the energy to what works, and mostly to what feels good. You have been shown this many times throughout your human history; now, as you embody the New Energy of the New Earth as evolved human beings, it will become more automatic to shift out of the emotions of upset, anger, hurt, resentment, and frustration to support, self-accountability, and cooperation—thus creating harmony and joy in your everyday interactions.

You feel the energy instantly when it is not serving you or others, and you also now have a greater awareness and capacity to shift that energy to what does serve. It truly is a choice, Dear Ones, a conscious choice to move freely in the New Energy unencumbered by old programming, old beliefs, old karma, old ways of being that have been imposed on you by whoever or whatever. It does not matter, and does not have to be analyzed or figured out, just acknowledged and shifted. You being in joy and loving creation is what is available to you in a more cognitive way in this new energy, but of course, it still is a choice on your part, no matter what someone else is choosing.

Each time you choose joy, you amplify your energy field exponentially. Each time you choose love, you amplify your energy field exponentially. Each time you see the Light in yourself or in someone else, you amplify your energy field exponentially. And science is showing you that a strong energy field creates a healthy body and mind, so you are supporting your own health by choosing these higher vibrational energies, as well as supporting the health of all of those you interact with personally. And of course, each balanced human beneficially affects the whole, not just your Earth but the Universe, so we support you to embody the powerful Light Energy that is available for the choosing.

Messages of HOPE from "US" (United Souls of Heaven and Earth)

Energetic Groundwork Being Laid

July 28, 2013

Dearest Beautiful Beings of Light,

In our recent transmissions, the focus has been on energy. We will continue with this theme as it is one of the most important things to understand that will assist you in these next few years. As we have said before, and as you are seeing for yourselves, your scientists are making great breakthroughs in being able to explain energy in quantum terms, rather than chemical terms, to show you what not only is possible, but what is actually happening on your Earth.

Many now understand what we mean when we say "the energetic groundwork is being laid," as they can feel it in their bodies, and then are able to see the reflection in circumstances in their lives as well as the world, and vice versa. As an example: purification through use of high-intensity light energy is a scientific understanding that is also happening within your bodies (i.e., hot flashes). As uncomfortable as they may feel, they are purifying your biology and enhancing your already powerful energy field.

As in any building process, it is important to start from the ground up. Even though many of you are looking to the Universe for that enhancement or restructuring, it is actually being laid in your Mother Earth and being reverberated through you as the conduits of Light that are forming the Light Grid connecting *All That Is*. We know that feels pretty big, though it actually is a natural process that is happening whether you are aware of it or not. With so many of you being sensitive to energy, more so now than ever (and will continue to be enhanced), it is important to understand the significance of taking good care of your biological health as well as your spiritual health.

Your spiritual awareness is what will really keep you centred and balanced in this New Energy. Explore what that is for you as there are many possible ways to experience spiritual energy, though really just *one* source. Share your experiences of how you feel energy in your body as well as your environment. The Universe is communicating with you *all* the time, in so many different ways. Being willing and aware is the key. You are being shown *much* at this time that is the foundation for what is to come.

Messages of HOPE from "US" (United Souls of Heaven and Earth)

Being in the Flow of Who You Are

August 11, 2013

Dearest Beautiful Beings of Light,

As you give more energy to your magnificence and less energy to your doubts, guess what happens, Dear Ones? You create more magnificence. You create many more possibilities. You create awareness. You create more harmony. You create more cooperation.

Each time that you give your energy to magnificence, and each time you choose to withdraw your energy from doubt, you are expanding exponentially. It is E E—the first letters of those two words, *expanding exponentially*, and when you use that vibration of the two E's, you create *ease*. Words themselves create great energy, depending on their interpretation; but pure sound, if you just take the sounds of the letters, has the greatest impact on you. So as you move through your day, Dear Ones, be aware of the sounds that you hear, as well as the sounds that you make. By taking a certain word and expressing that word, you are creating a sound vibration that is either going to have a beneficial impact or a possibly not-so-beneficial impact for you.

Being aware of the E sound right now is creating ease for yourself, and every time you use an E word with that harmonic resonance, you are creating more harmony within your systems. And that is one of our purposes for being here at this time: first of all, to bring through the vibration of *joy* but also *harmony*. As you are in harmony with yourself, and even as you say that word, you will feel the vibration happen within your body, to feel the harmony within your body. Because, remember, the body is the vehicle, and the more you can create harmony from within, the harmony shows up from without.

One of the vibrations we are here at this time to transmit to you is *harmony*, and as you say that word to yourself, even within your mind ... *harmony* ... you feel it in your body. It has a flow. It has a connection. It is very interrelated with the infinity. The infinity creates flow. It creates movement. It creates connectedness. So when you are in harmony with yourself, you are in harmony with others, you are in harmony with the environment, you are in harmony with the Universe, you are in harmony with your planet, you are in harmony with the animals, you are in harmony with *All That Is*. That is one of the energies we are transmitting that will amplify your magnificence because, again, it is energy. As you let go of aspects and personality characteristics, you will understand more and more about the energies that you are embodying, the energies that you are exuding; that is what it is all about at this time. It is a beautiful opportunity to be in the flow with yourself and others.

Messages of HOPE from "US" (United Souls of Heaven and Earth)

Emanating Your Mastery of the Light
September 11, 2013

Dearest Beautiful Beings of Light,

Many of the things that you have seen in your world that you would label as unbearable, as disastrous, as tragic—all of those things that you as humans would use to describe an event that happened on September 11th—we are asking you today to lift that vibration. It is for those of you in this dimension to raise up the vibration so this does not have to be a continuous pattern. It is holding the vibration of love and joy and peace and harmony and cooperation and all of the things, even to the point of bliss.

This date of September 11th, on which your bodies and your minds may be remembering something that did not seem to be of love and joy and peace and harmony, was a catalyst to move humanity forward in great bounds and leaps. There are other events out there in your world that you have perceived as tragic or unnecessary; you are moving into a time that it is absolutely true that you will not have to manifest what you would call tragedies for your enlightenment.

That is the piece that is shifting quickly for each and every one of you. We honour you and implore you and encourage you to lift up your thoughts, to lift up your vibration. So it is to all of you who are experiencing any kind of challenge or worry at this point: rise above it, rise above it, rise above it! Take your energy up. Always be conscious of choosing the highest possible vibration that you can be in, whether it is in your own thought process in your mind or a conversation with another person.

You already know this; we are just reiterating and helping you to take it to the next level of energy, and it is truly about energy. You are learning more and more about vibration, and energy, and frequency, and as you allow yourself that greater awareness, Dear Ones, the shifts will happen quicker. What you have been experiencing in the energy fields are choice points. You will come to many choice points that ask: What are you going to do with this? What are you going to focus on? How are you going to interpret this? What is your perception? What is the energy that you are giving your energy to? What is the energy you are bringing into your awareness? What is the energy you are bringing into your body? What is the energy you are exuding?

It is a constant state of awareness for each and every one of you to be in; it is all in Divine perfection. As you feel that, first of all about yourself—that you *are* Divine perfection, and that you *are in* Divine perfection, and that *you exude* Divine perfection—that will be the experience that you create. Lift your mind and your energy to a higher level and also to a more inward level of that higher vibration that you carry within you, because now you are ready for it.

It is truly a marker moment as we bring in, and exude, and transmit, and hold, and share the energy of 11. The energy of 11 is one of the most powerful frequencies on your earth at this time. It truly is the Master energy. It truly is the Christ Consciousness. It truly is a powerful manifestation energy. As you tune in very

Messages of HOPE from "US" (United Souls of Heaven and Earth)

intensely and consciously to the energy vibrations of 11, you are now able to emanate the energy of your Mastery and of the 11 in a great capacity.

Messages of HOPE from "US" (United Souls of Heaven and Earth)

Staying Balanced in an Unbalanced World

October 4, 2013

Dearest Beautiful Beings of Light,

As you are well aware, there is great dichotomy in your world right now with many extremes, and you are feeling them within your own mind, emotions, and energy fields. These extremes, internally or externally, are all part of the energetic re-balancing that has occurred as you passed through the Fall Equinox alignment.

When energy realigns in the Universe, it can often have the opposite effect as it pulses to the third-dimensional realm; that is what you are experiencing at this moment in time. It is up to you, and only you, how you respond, react to, or manage this energy. You are witnessing in the world at large, and also for many of you personally, the next phase of your awakening, and the now even-greater necessity to trust your own inner knowing of what is best for you. When you veer away from that inner knowing and your personal truth, it becomes instantly painful, emotionally and physically.

At the same time, you are having more profound and instantaneous experiences of inner alignment, and shifting discordant energies that you may have dwelt on for much longer. You are aligning with your own higher vibrational knowing, and it is speaking louder and louder through physical and emotional symptoms if you choose not to listen. When you choose to listen to that higher knowing of what is possible and what is serving you, and of course serving others in the process, you can feel your inner core come into balance and harmony, and the angst dissipates much more quickly than it has before.

Truly, what you choose to give your thought and energy to will either bring you more into balance or take you more out of balance. Each time you do or think something that creates that inner balance or peace, you are making a difference in everything and everyone in your environment, as well as the world as a whole. What creates balance in your life? Make it a higher priority, and all will benefit from your renewed energy, perspective, and well-being.

We have said before that from the greatest chaos comes the greatest harmony, so we encourage you to know that you *are* creating harmony for yourself and your world—it is just re-balancing. And you are being shown the opposite of what you want so you can make a conscious choice rather than just going along with what was. Honouring yourself and knowing you are much greater than any external circumstance in your life will create the inner balance to take the actions that will create the outer balance in those discordant circumstances. To do so, you are at this time receiving much energetic support from all the realms of the Universe.

Messages of HOPE from "US" (United Souls of Heaven and Earth)

Transitions, Changes and the Unknown
November 27 2013

Dearest Beautiful Beings of Light,

It is with great joy that we energetically support you as so many of you are going through great changes in your life, transitioning from who you once were to who you really are. That may sound a little confusing as the truth of your magnificence is revealed to you piece by piece, layer by layer, circumstance by circumstance, experience by experience to show you not only what is possible but what *is!*

Making changes in your life circumstances and moving into the unknown is one of the most unsettling things for humans, and we applaud those of you who are just doing it! The unknown does not have to be a scary place; it is the place of creation, the void. As you move into the coming time of the Winter Solstice, it creates the darkness to shroud you so you can go inside your being, inside of your knowing where all is being created in perfect Divine alignment. Walking through the dark, literally or figuratively, not only takes courage; however it gives you the opportunity to more consciously tap into your sensing—not just your physical senses, but your spiritual senses.

It is your spiritual sense that will support you in these times of change, these times of transitioning from a world of fear to a world of love and joy. What is *your* spiritual sense? What is your connection to something greater than you know in this moment, which is ever expanding? Opening to a spiritual connection, whatever that is for you, is of great benefit to you as human beings as you energetically transition to Light Beings. Energetically it is happening, whether you are aware of it or not. Creating a spiritual connection, a sacred space within yourself, will support all the transitions you are experiencing, whether big or seemingly insignificant. Change is just a shift of energy, and is very necessary at this time as you are clearing your energy and are raising your vibration.

You are "spirit-u-all"—*all* of you living on your Earth right now, no matter how you have lived your life up to this point. You are spirit in a physical body, and it is through your physical body that your spirit can have the most beneficial impact on the transitions that are happening in your life and your Earth. Take quiet time to feel how spirit moves through you, expresses through you, *is* you! It is all in the feeling. The unknown is unknown for a reason. It is shown to you in moments that align with your truth and with the Universal energy of creation. If you knew what is possible for you to create, you would never have another thought of fear, worry, guilt, or limitedness and constriction. You would only feel excitement.

Embracing change and the unknown—allowing the transition from struggle to ease, from chaos to harmony, from lack to abundance, from conflict to peace, from worry to trust, and from fear to love and joy—is the greatest gift you can give yourselves and those you care about. It is already laid into the energy field of the Earth and into your DNA. It is now just a matter of allowing it to activate within your own being, one breath at a time, one moment at a time. That is all it takes.

Messages of HOPE from "US" (United Souls of Heaven and Earth)

Wrapping Up the Old and Beginning the New

December 31, 2013

Dearest Beautiful Beings of Light,

You are being given a gift this day of energetic alignment with *all* that you have been, *all* that you are, and *all* that you will be. As you read these words, allow the energy and vibration that we transmit to you to support you in transition from questioning to higher knowing, from struggle to ease, from density to Light—and, most importantly, from fear to love. Just feel it!

As you wrap up this impactful year of 2013, take time to wrap up the challenges and experiences you have had, like a gift with a beautiful golden bow on top. See it *all* as a gift that showed you without a doubt your strengths, your courage, your creativity, your adaptability *and* the beneficial effect your radiance as a Light Being has had on others. Take time this day, as your clock moves towards midnight, to acknowledge the gift that you are to others. Your radiance in this world has a greater impact than you will ever know, and as you acknowledge the effects that you are aware of, big or small, you expand that magnificent energy to encompass more influence and more shift in your world to peace and harmony.

Much of the old programming that has been the operating system within your minds and bodies has been dissolved, deleted, and restored to a much higher frequency; as we said in one of our previous teleconference channels: hit your restart button and you will be amazed at what shows up in your life. This coming year of 2014 has possibilities that you have not yet imagined. By being open to anything new, you will allow doors to open that will create many new experiences for you to express the beautiful energy of creation that is encoded within your cells, now primed and ready to come forth.

You will start to notice that you are much more aware of being centred and grounded than has been possible for those traveling the spiritual path and living the human life up to this point. Your heightened consciousness in each experience will be an automatic clue, allowing you to shift energy instantly to what is better serving you and those around you. You will start to feel much less constriction in your bodies, your minds and, mostly, in your hearts. Of course, the result is embracing new experiences with enthusiasm, passion, trust and openness.

As we said in our previous written transmission, your senses are what have been upgraded in this past year's intense energetic alignment. Your Spiritual sense is being restored, and it is just a matter of owning it. It is who you are. You are a Divine Being of Light—always have been, always will be—and now you have more ability to express it in the world you live in. Do it with joy as you move into this year of power and Light!

Messages of HOPE from "US" (United Souls of Heaven and Earth)

Perception of Energy

January 14, 2014

Dearest Beautiful Beings of Light,

There is change going on within the core of your being, within the cellular structure, within the DNA; this is well known to all of you on a spiritual path. And what that is also creating, of course, is change in your external world.

As you perceive something as chaotic, difficult, challenging, that is what you bring into your reality; as you perceive energy as supportive, beneficial, easeful, that is what your body attunes to. There are many attunements happening at this time, and as you stay in your centre, in the core of your Being, in the core of your knowing, you allow your perception of energy to raise its frequency, to raise the frequency above what has been.

Your perception of energy is your empowerment, and we are going to say that one again: Your perception of energy *is* your empowerment! As you perceive things supporting you, as you perceive events aligning, as you perceive beneficial outcomes, as you perceive all whom you see as Divine Beings, as you perceive yourself as a powerful being-creator, all of those energies get amplified. And, of course, the first shift that is the most powerful is the shift in perception of yourself, the shift in knowing that truth of who you are.

It is not that others do not perceive energy; it is about *how* they perceive energy. It time for each of you to uplift your awareness into a higher knowing of what energy *really* is, and the power of it, and how to create with it, how to create with this *New Energy*. Because of the shifts that you have already gone through, the changes at the DNA level, your power to perceive energy *has been amplified*.

We are here to tell you, there is nothing to do. Just be with it, accept the grandness of it, the amplification of the knowing that truly, *truly* all is well. We have said in many, many channels before: ALL IS WELL, Dear Ones! No matter what is happening in your life or someone else's life, all is truly well. The energies are creating something absolutely magnificent for each and every one of you to embrace, for you to integrate, for you to embody the truth, the newness, the crystallization. There is so much crystal energy available that is a very fine tuned energy. And there will be more information to come about the new abilities that you are able to create with the crystal energy, that, again, you have already encoded into your cells. That is part of the coding that is being amplified for each and every one of you to then connect at that higher dimensional level of the integration of *All That Is* from *All That Was!*.

Messages of HOPE from "US" (United Souls of Heaven and Earth)

Do You REALLY Want More Joy?

February 2, 2014

Dearest Beautiful Beings of Light,

This may seem like a silly question at this time, with so many challenges in your world and in your personal lives; however, we invite you to ponder this question as there are so many possibilities available to each of you in the New Energy of 2014. More and more, it truly is up to you what you create. By your own intentions you have come through an intense phase of clearing and un-densifying at a cellular level so that your DNA can be reconnected (just like wiring). We have said before it is happening for all humans; the difference in how easy or how challenging it is for each of you is in your consciousness.

There has been much discovered and written about your consciousness. There are many experts out there sharing their information to trigger or spark the knowing that has been embedded in your physical body since the beginning of time as you know it. That time is *now*! There have been so many spiritual teachers who have helped prepare the way, helped prepare your bodies, your minds, your hearts and the energy fields of your Earth to literally be turned on for the quantum leap that is about to take place. There has been much intricate, as well as intensive, energy recalibration occurring on levels known (and unknown) to you, which has prepared you energetically to contain the higher vibration of JOY. Our question to you is: *Do you feel* you are ready for it? What would happen if you just said *yes*?

As you always have the choice in what you create in your life, this is a profound question for you to embrace as we in the other realms can only send the energy, recalibrate the fields, activate at cellular levels, support you and love you. The rest is up to you in what you give your attention to that allows your consciousness to expand or to contract. It always has been this way—though now, with the acceleration of the vibrational fields, your thoughts and your choices carry more weight than ever before. We know many of you are having moments of unexplained feelings of joy, even though your life may not be exactly as you would like it or hoped it would be at this point in time; this is just a prelude to what is possible.

All of your senses (again, those known to you and those unknown to you) are also being upgraded to match the higher vibrational energy accessible to you now. That is one of the reasons some of you feel the need to shut down or to dull or mask your feelings in some way as they feel bigger than your body or your mind can contain. We assure you that you absolutely can not only contain this energy in your bodies, you are here to share it, vibrationally, with others.

Take a moment to imagine a world where every person knew, without a shadow of a doubt, that experiencing JOY was why they are here on Earth. Can you feel how it would change how you experience everything? Happy people make conscious choices; conscious choices create more joy. Can you feel where we are going with this? Let yourself play with these thoughts, and ENJOY the journey.

Messages of HOPE from "US" (United Souls of Heaven and Earth)

Adaptability in the New Energies

March 3, 2014

Dearest Beautiful Beings of Light,

It is with great joy that we send these transmissions to you through word and through vibration as vibrational awareness is an important key in your ability to adapt to what is happening in these New Energies. And even the term "New Energies" is all about vibration as it truly is expanding each moment. There are new energies available on your planet now that have never been accessible before—they are of a higher frequency and therefore require a certain amount of adapting to. It will take more adapting for some people and less adapting for others, depending on many different circumstances—for example, receptivity, ability to centre oneself, awareness of a grander scheme, a higher vision, a willingness to trust and an assuredness from within.

The influx of Cosmic energies being beamed to your Earth at this time requires you to be able to go with what is happening in the moment without being attached to what you think should be happening, either in your own life or in the world. As things are shifting and changing at such an accelerated rate now, your ability to adapt will be what gives you the greatest peace as well as the greatest empowerment. Note we said *em*powerment, not *power*, as your personal power is being activated from within; it is this personal empowerment that is giving you the strong base from which to adapt to anything that happens in the moment.

Human beings were created with a powerful sense of adaptability, and that sense is now being called into action as the transformations take place in your world and in your personal lives. We said in our transmission on February 21st that there were new possibilities that opened on that day, and these new possibilities will require a degree of adaptability that you have not had to call upon as yet. We want to assure you: you are very capable of adapting to New Energies and circumstances coming your way.

One of the greatest challenges for humans has been to truly accept what you have always hoped for, wished for, dreamed of, and envisioned, once it actually starts to show up in your reality. In the past, it has been much easier for you to adapt to difficult circumstances than to adapt to wonderful circumstances that come your way—always feeling like you don't really know what to do with it or trust it. As a result, the energy wanes and you go back to your comfort zone of adapting to something that may be less than optimal, not really what you had hoped for and definitely not your dream come true. Because if it really came true, what then? You would be in unfamiliar territory—the unknown!

You have had so many years—eons, actually—of adapting to hardship that it is a total shift, a reprogramming that is happening for you to adapt to *joy*, the energy of joy, the frequency of joy, the vibration of joy, the feeling of joy, and the circumstances that are created as a result of accepting that joy is possible—yes, you really *can* adapt to this energy, these New Energies that are being beamed to your Earth from many different dimensions. There are many circumstances that unfold in human existence that are viewed as not joyful, and what we are saying is that is just the way it has been up to this point. As you start to adapt physically, mentally, emotionally and spiritually to these New Energies, your external circumstances will start to shift from hardship to ease, from fear to love, and from pain to joy.

You all have the opportunity now to adapt to a New World that has been created (note we said *has* been created) in the vibrations of joy, love, harmony, and peace as you leave the old energies and vibrations in the past—no need to keep bringing them forward with you as you travel the road of your current life. The energy of the New World is here NOW. Are you ready to adapt to it? It is easier than you think.

Messages of HOPE from "US" (United Souls of Heaven and Earth)

Accelerated Transmutation Phase
April 4, 2014

Dearest Beautiful Beings of Light,

You have entered a new phase of transmutation of old cell memory that is now possible because of the groundwork that has been laid by all of your intentions for a more harmonic, peaceful world. And this energy of harmony is being created from the inside out. You may have noticed over the past few weeks, particularly since the Spring Equinox, alignment that things have once again sped up while at the same time slowed down. It feels like everything is happening and nothing is happening all at the same time. That is because of the acceleration that you have engaged in as part of the process of cleaning out the old cell memory that has been fixated in the body. We use the word *fixated* very specifically because your thoughts and memories have been in an almost non-moveable energy that now is being blasted through.

And again, we specifically use the words *blasted through,* just like dynamiting through the rocks of a mountain to create a roadway in your 3D world. The Cosmic energies are blasting through the rock-solid energies of old memories that no longer serve you, shattering them to little pieces that are much more easily discarded than trying to haul away a mountain. Once your cell memory has been blasted, you will notice waves of thoughts of old situations coming out of nowhere for no particular reason or not having been stimulated by something that you are aware of. That is because you have given permission and much intent on your spiritual awakening path for it to be easier. Releasing old, stuck cell memory in pails full of gravel, rather than a truckload of huge pieces of rock, will be much more effective now in lightening the load, so to speak, in your emotional, mental, and physical body.

So when you feel the blast of energy breaking up the fixated energies within you, give thanks to your Spirit for knowing what is best for you and accelerating the process of clearing in manageable amounts—and we want to emphasize the words *manageable amounts*, because that is the truth, even though it may not feel like it. Just imagine many unseen beings in an assembly line taking away the pails of gravel to be used elsewhere in the building of something much more useful to humanity; that is what transmutation is. It doesn't just disappear, because everything is energy. Your cell memory is being transmuted into something much more useful in the building of the New World.

The month of April will be an extremely accelerated transmutation month for *all*, and those of you who have a greater awareness of the Cosmic process will also have a greater acceptance and easier transition. We commend you on your dedication to raising your consciousness and perceiving what is happening on energetic levels. We support you to share what you know with others as it will soothe and affirm what they are experiencing as well. As we have said in previous transmissions, 2014 is a powerful year of change, showing you what is now possible in the higher frequencies. All is well!

Messages of HOPE from "US" (United Souls of Heaven and Earth)

Change Takes Courage
May 14, 2014

Dearest Beautiful Beings of Light,

The energy of this day (1+4=5), this month (fifth month), and this phase of awakening is about change, and change does not come easily to most humans. You would rather stay in what you know, even though it may not be what you want. If it is not what you want, it will become more and more uncomfortable until you are ultimately forced to change. That does not necessarily mean change your life circumstances as in living situation, relationships, or geography, though that may well happen for many. What it *does* mean is having the courage to change on the inside, to shift the thoughts, beliefs and mainly perceptions of yourself!

As you feel the intensity of the full moon of this day and the few following days, be gentle with yourself and with others as the stuff that is buried will come to the surface one way or another, through dreams, through self-deprecating or judgmental thoughts, through conversations or even through confrontations. We spoke in our previous channel of the new phase of transmutation of old cell memory that you have entered, which is facilitating the creation of harmony from the inside out. It is to be able to look at what is working (or not working) for you in your life from a non-critical, neutral, objective point of view. To go below the surface to what is really happening, to what you are really feeling, is critical at this point of your energetic clearing and upgrading. "The truth will set you free" is not just a pretty saying. It carries a great source of energetic shifting that leads to greater well-being on all levels, though you will feel it instantaneously on a physical level as relief first of all, and then clarity and empowerment to take necessary actions.

To admit your truth does take courage, as it can bring up many emotions and reactions. It takes a certain level of emotional and spiritual maturity to be accountable for your own feelings and actions and to make adjustments, as necessary, when they are not creating the result you desire in your life. You can choose to ignore, or even to tightly hold onto, what is not working for you or not serving the highest good for all, though it will get more and more uncomfortable at this time of accelerated evolution. There is much support for you in this phase of transmutation to acknowledge your truth, of allowing that spiritual aspect of yourself to have more intentional acknowledgement, and to truly let your Spirit guide you!

The melding of Spirit, your Divine Essence, with your physicality is a powerful process that is fully underway for all. Consciously choosing it and being accountable for your part of the process makes it a much more empowered and joyous journey! We in the other dimensions are here at this time, on this powerful day of the gathering of Enlightened Beings (referring to Wesak, the full moon festival each year where it is said the Buddha and other Enlightened Beings appear in the Himalayas to bless the world) to support that journey.

Messages of HOPE from "US" (United Souls of Heaven and Earth)

You Have What It Takes!
June 14, 2014

Dearest Beautiful Beings of Light,

This is a profound message that we give to you this day as it is the *truth*! The truth has been the energy focus of our transmissions of late, and we are giving you a big one in these words:

You *do* have what it takes to manage your own energy in the ever-changing rhythms and circumstances of your life and the world. The rapid acceleration of change has left many feeling they are not capable of handling the shifts, whether they be shifts in thinking, emotions, finances, relationships, health and well-being, world events or whatever. And we are here to tell you that you absolutely *can*. You are made up from the same stuff as the Universe. You have within you everything that ever was or ever will be.

It is just a matter of accepting that you are more powerful than you have ever known, that you have access to anything that your mind can conceive of (and even that which it is not yet able to conceive). That your Spirit is ever present, ever loving and ever guiding you to raise your awareness, lift your energy and vibration, clear your emotional garbage ... to be free!

To be free does not mean you go floating off somewhere in the ether, or just go from place to place in your world without any direction. It means you are free to make choices and enjoy this life, right here, right now! By knowing you have it all deep down at the core of your being, you resonate that energy out in everything you think, say, and do—and, voila, there it is! Whatever the *it* is that you focus on, it shows up.

You have what it takes to surmount any obstacle that presents, and it presents to show you that you have what it takes. Isn't that an interesting merry-go-round? Though you do not have to be on the merry-go-round, you can actually choose to be on the merry-go-*forward*. Do you feel that? It doesn't make you so dizzy. It inspires you, motivates you. It is time to get off the merry-go-round, step onto the merry-go-*forward*, and start creating with joy! You have done lots of clearing of energy, so let the ride get easier for you now. Get to know the happy you, and you will be shown how it is done . . . no more quandary, much more clarity.

You have an inner strength that bars none. You came into this life with it. It is always there. It just gets a little buried and ignored sometimes. You are made of tough stuff. Now is the time to acknowledge it, embrace it, and let it shine forth, you beautiful Beings of Light!

Messages of HOPE from "US" (United Souls of Heaven and Earth)

Truth Takes Courage
July 14, 2014

Dearest Beautiful Beings of Light,

Living in truth is the greatest act of courage a human being can take on in this lifetime. To be brave and confident enough to not only speak what you know to be true for you but to truly live it is the energy of the New Earth being anchored through you. By doing so, you are creating a world of authenticity where it is not only okay to be who you are but encouraged rather than squelched. Each little expression of truth from the heart builds an energy field that expands to influence the more complicated situations in your life in beneficial ways as it clears energy.

You are pioneers at the edge of so many amazing breakthroughs in human conditioning that now is the time you will see the powerful results of shifting your way of being to be the example of authentic, heart-centred expression. With so many Cosmic alignments facilitating deep cleansing and clearing of old patterns and cell memory of late, you are questioning what is your truth at this point. That is okay, Dear Ones, because with each shift of energy, the *New You*, and the New World, become more crystal clear. We specifically use the word *crystal* as it is one of the energies that is being emanated to you and through you. Crystal is a high-quality, refined energy that allows for clear viewing (and clear hearing).

When you see things clearly, you are able to make decisions more easily and with more confidence and empowerment, knowing there is a greater purpose to your actions no matter how it is being interpreted or judged by others, or even by yourself.

The old conditioning that has kept you restricted and limited in your thinking and your life circumstances is literally melting away; that is why we refer to you as pioneers. You are stepping out in unprecedented ways, with unprecedented information, and with unprecedented ways of being that are changing your world. You have felt it deep at your core, and now you have more access to this internal knowing to actually live it day to day in your personal interactions with each other. Many on a spiritual path have experienced expressing your truth with one another to find that it was easier than you thought, as well as very freeing. Energy shifted instantaneously and gave you the courage to embrace and speak truth with others in your lives—those that may not have been easy to communicate with before or have an understanding of where you are coming from.

Trust what you feel and what you know, as the recent alignment on the 7-7-7 facilitated an expansion of your senses to encompass so much more than has been possible thus far in your sensory being. Your energy systems have gone through profound upgrades to support you in this next phase of expression of who you really are! Embrace and enjoy this beautiful expression in yourself and others!

Messages of HOPE from "US" (United Souls of Heaven and Earth)

Emotional Balance in Unsettled Energies
August 14, 2014

Dearest Beautiful Beings of Light,

There is much unsettled energy on your Earth at this time, and that is actually beneficial as it is moving you out of the density and limitations you have been in since the beginning of your human existence. However, it is now time for you to take more focused intention in your own emotional balance and well-being. For as you do that for yourself, you are doing a great service to your Earth and all her peoples. Your balanced emotional energy is a strong resonant field that reverberates out to others in your life, to the mass consciousness as well as to the Universal field of information that is available to all dimensions physical and non-physical.

How do I do that, you ask? You do it with conscious intent, with a deep *knowing* that it *is* possible! That you are powerful beings of creation that are here at this time for exactly that purpose, to use your innate abilities to create peace within, as well as peace without. As you hold loving, beneficial thoughts in your mind and in your heart, the Universal field responds instantly to those vibrations, even though you may not see the manifestations of those thoughts right away, or in the way that you thought they would show up. Trusting in the Divine orchestration to organize the details and then taking inspired action keeps you in alignment with the energy flow and out of the chaos of fear and drama.

Many of you are experiencing extremes right now—extremes of life experiences that are helping you to come back into balance. It is like the fulcrum swinging from one extreme to the other, eventually settling in the middle in stillness. Balance is in the core of your being; it is not in the external world. Your emotions are showing you what is not working for you, as well as what *is* working for you. It is just energy, and energy moves in waves, never in a straight line. As you are experiencing emotional waves, know that no matter what situation, Cosmic or personal, may be influencing the fluctuation of these waves of energy in your life, *you* are always the one in charge of how you manage these waves of energy. You always have not only the choice of how you react to them but the absolute capability of finding the balance from within to be able to use the energy waves in very beneficial ways rather than letting them immobilize you.

Surround yourself with people who know that they are capable of creating emotional balance as they will reflect back to you that they know you are capable as well. You are all mirrors for one another, so make conscious choices in who and what you are letting be reflected back to you. We have said before that you all have what it takes to move through these times of chaos and to create a world of peace, harmony, joy and love; it begins with creating that from within in your own personal life. It *is* possible, and you *are* doing it—hold that thought in your mind!

Unsettled Energies Are Catalysts For Change

September 14, 2014

Dearest Beautiful Beings of Light,

As you are well aware, there is much unsettled energy in your world: in global situations; in weather conditions; in personal relationships; in your physical chemistry; in your minds. These unsettled energies *are* the catalysts for change. It is in the shake-up that you wake up!

As you view the chaos out there, bless it and celebrate it as it is literally blowing up the old energy, like dynamiting through the rocks (old dense energy) to create greater access (new highway) to higher awareness. It is from this higher awareness that the change you so desire in your world can be accomplished.

When you see chaos in any situation, minor or catastrophic, bless it, Dear Ones, rather than cursing it or being debilitated by it. That will send out a powerful vibration that will assist the necessary change rather than resist it, or continue to feed the unwanted situation. You are much more powerful beings than you give yourself credit for. You have the power within your mind, body, and energy field to change the world as you know it. It is through energy and by just believing that it is so! We have said before that you are the conduits of the Light that is being anchored on your Earth; as this Light gets anchored and emanated through you, it stirs things up—it cleans house, and cleaning house can get messy and uncomfortable.

Being uncomfortable is one of the symptoms of impending change. You have seen it before in your lives and felt the benefit of the changes that ensued. During these times of the Great Shift, it is just on a much grander scale than you have yet to experience, and it is the unknown that creates the greatest discomfort for most of you. Remember, it is in the unknown, in the great void, that creation happens—and creation *is* happening on a grand scale in these present moments. As more of you allow yourself to be comfortable with the unknown, and hold the vision for what you *do* want, it is creating a powerful emanation of benevolent energy that the Universe *is* responding to, even though you may not see tangible results in this moment. Just know that the New Energy field for the Earth is in place; each time you send benevolent energy thoughts out from your mind and your body, it powers that field to override the old programs and conditioning.

Your physical chemistry is going through immense change that is also creating much uncomfortableness, like you want to jump out of your skin. We encourage you to love and soothe your body as if it were a scared child or animal, and assure it that you will take good care of it through these times It will require very different foods and nutrients and more rest as it goes through the fluctuations of energy. Honour that, listen to your body—it is very wise and is the vehicle for your personal gift to this world; that gift is YOU in all your glory and magnificence!

Tension Can Create Spiritual Growth
October 14, 2014

Dearest Beautiful Beings of Light,

Spiritual growth, whether you know it or not, *is* happening for everyone on your planet. Spiritual growth can be defined in many different ways, depending on your belief system, though it truly comes down to whether you are embracing and exuding the energy of LOVE. Very simple!

There are many opportunities unfolding in your world for your spiritual growth to expand in ways that you may not have ever been aware of before, or have not had the emotional maturity to embrace. Tension is one of the energies that gives you an impetus to expand your spiritual growth through the choices you make when experiencing tense situations.

When tension is applied to an object it can make the object that it is affecting stronger—or it can break it. You have that choice now with the tensions in your personal lives, as well as in your world. There are more and more tense moments and tense situations now because you have, at some level, given yourself permission for the greatest spiritual growth possible. You can see everything in Divine order, allowing you to make empowered choices and become stronger in knowing who you are; or you can feel that the tension you are experiencing is breaking your Spirit. It is all in how you look at it, and it is all in what you choose to put back out there into the energy fields, which influence everything and everyone.

Think of a tense situation in your life right now and ask yourself, *How is it serving me?* Are you aware of how you are *being* in it? Because you are the only one who can expand that or contract that. The energy you are putting out is either expanding your spiritual growth or diminishing it, and you know which one feels good. This month of October, with its Cosmic alignments and eclipses, will provide you with many opportunities to be aware of who you are as a Divine Being, and of the lower vibrational energies that you are now ready to release. It is just a matter of being willing. You don't need to know all the hows—just be willing to use tension as a way to shift from what you don't want and what is not serving you, to what you *do* want and what *is* serving you, as this will serve the greater whole as well, because you are all connected.

What happens to one is experienced by all, so as you shift and clear your own stuff, you do it for many as it then reverberates through the resonant energy field for all to feel at some level. It is all just energy and how it can serve you! So choose LOVE—for yourself first, and then for anywhere else you experience tension in your life, and in your world. It will serve you well!

Messages of HOPE from "US" (United Souls of Heaven and Earth)

Shifting Old Energy
November 14, 2014

Dearest Beautiful Beings of Light,

Shifting old energy has been the focus of many beings in both the physical and non-physical world. There are many of you who are very intent on releasing what has kept you limited, and embracing what expands you, and we want to assure you that you *are* doing it! Even though you may still be experiencing situations in your life that feel like old energy, you are seeing things and acting upon them from completely new energies that support you to have a higher and broader perspective.

This expanded perspective takes in the whole and is being embraced now, because it is time! There has been much preparation for this time right now that is allowing you the bigger vision—not just for your world but for yourself, first and foremost. As we have said many times before, within every cell of your being is contained everything, and you are now able to see, feel, and sense that on so many levels. There are many questions that you have had over the last few decades that are now being answered. You are being shown the reasons for so many things that have happened in your personal lives that now are empowering you to shift energy—to shift your physical energy, to shift your emotional energy, to shift your mental energy, and to shift your spiritual energy . . . and you now feel it instantly when you do. So the shifts that you make create the inspiration, motivation, and the template to do it more consistently. And you *are!*

We really want to emphasize those three words: AND YOU ARE! It is important for you to believe, not only to keep your confidence bolstered but to keep your vibration high. Keeping your vibration high means knowing without a shadow of a doubt and feeling your connection to your Divine Essence, and letting that knowing, that feeling, direct everything you think, say, and do in any situation, easy or challenging. It is the challenging situations, Dear Ones, that are allowing you to make the greatest shifts of old dense energy. They can be transformed in the blink of an eye simply by choosing to see them from a broader perspective that allows you to embody the higher vibration of love and compassion. In doing so, you become a human vessel for the Light of the Universe to shine on Earth.

As you have just passed through the powerful portal and activation of the 11:11, you will now begin to feel the shifts of old energy that *have* occurred these past few months. Your body will feel lighter and your mind more clear. The 11 energy is about your mastery and your alignment with the Christ consciousness to support you as you share your mastery of the new incoming energies with grace and ease—and mostly with JOY!

Messages of HOPE from "US" (United Souls of Heaven and Earth)

Conscious Creation
December 14, 2014

Dearest Beautiful Beings of Light,

This time of year is ripe with so many possibilities as you come to the close of one of the most powerful cleansing and clearing years in human evolution! We do not say that lightly, because we know the depths that some of you have gone to this year to resolve, dissolve, shift, transmute, transform and transcend old energy that has been weighing you down and slowing down your progress of stepping into your mission. Just know, Dear Ones, it has all been for a reason—both the challenges you have had in your life to this point, and the timing of the clearing of it at a cellular level.

There is a great Divine plan unfolding that each and every one of you is a significant part of, whether you believe that or not. When you are aware of your own accountability as being a contributor, making conscious choices becomes not only very empowering but moves to the top of your list of priorities, thus your awareness and your intentions come even more into play as your life unfolds. When you accept that you truly are a co-creator with Spirit, you will automatically slow down your thoughts and your doing-ness to tap into what you know feels right for you—even if it does not look like what others (or even you) think it should.

For these next few weeks, you are being bathed in Cosmic energies of Light and Love that are being emanated to your New Earth, as well as being emanated from your Earth as so many of you celebrate the season of the return of the Light and focus on peace on earth. As you do that, Dear Ones, you are consciously creating the new Earth . . . a world where you *can* live in peace, in harmony, and in joy! Know it to be true. Envision it, speak of it, and be conscious of what you are creating with your words, your thoughts, and your energy, as your power is expanding to be able to create instantly; manifestation is at your fingertips. Allow the energy that you put out to come from your heart, from that place deep inside that knows your own Divinity no matter what beliefs you were conditioned with growing up.

As you pass the threshold of 2014 to 2015, give great gratitude for what has unfolded in your life and the world, for it has been preparation for the phenomenal amount of Light that you are now able to hold within your physical being. This was not even remotely possibly for most of you before this point in time. Embrace the new energies with an open heart and an open mind as your mind will not believe it is possible. Your mind will want to default to the old ways of being, because they are familiar and accepted by those you have interacted with in your life until now. If you are reading our words, it means you are a way-shower, and it is time, Dear Ones, to do that consciously now, with intention to just BE the Light, BE the peace, BE the harmony, BE the joy and, most importantly, to BE the Love. .

The clearings and upgrades that you have experienced recently will make it easier to do that. You will experience fewer doubts or conflicts when you are accountable for and manage your own energy by being conscious of what it is that you are creating with your thoughts, words, and deeds as you move through your day minute by minute. You now have greater access to not only

Universal information but to higher vibrational energy that you can choose to embody at this time, which will greatly serve you personally, as well as your beautiful planet Earth. You are loved and supported by so many in the unseen realms, and it is up to you how much of this Divine Love you can accept. We are beaming it at you ... allow yourself to feel it and embody it as you consciously create the next phase of human evolution.

Messages of HOPE from "US" (United Souls of Heaven and Earth)

Are You Feeling the Shift?
January 15, 2015

Dearest Beautiful Beings of Light,

We ask you this question to help bring your awareness to what has taken place within you in the past few weeks. For some it may have been very subtle, though for many of the way-showers on Earth at this time, it has been a profound shift in being—a profound shift in experiencing your life and relations as well as your perceptions of your personal circumstances. The energy that was emanated to your Earth from the Cosmos recently anchored a new way of being through your cellular structure. This has been in process for many years now—the activation at a cellular level—and even though many of you heard about it, read about it, did your best to understand it, you only felt it in fleeting moments. Now you have the energetic ability to feel this shift of your cellular structure in more recognizable and more applicable ways that will continue to show you who you really are.

One such way is the feeling of inner peace in a more expanded way, an acceptance of what is—not always trying to push and control things to be the way you would like. As a result, you will be in your core energy and empowered to do exactly that, but on a grander scale. This year of 2015 in particular, as well as the next few years to come, have the greatest potential of manifestation that has yet been experienced by humankind. You have gone through bits and spurts of this energy of creation and manifestation; the difference now is that you have the ability to embody it, not just think it or act upon it. As a result, it becomes your way of being and shows up in tangible experiences where you will be saying, "Oh my goodness, I didn't expect it to unfold that way. That is way better than I had planned it!"

When that happens, it is resetting the old programming that had you always feeling like you had to work hard, had to push through whatever, and had to control people and situations to get what you wanted. That paradigm is done! There is no need to default back to it, even though it has been your habit. When that happens, as it will on a mental level, take a breath and allow yourself to go deeper, to your cellular level, and feel the shift that *has* occurred there, and let that New Energy come forward into your awareness. Allow the next thought, the next word, and the next action to come from that place . . . a place you actually know quite well as it is innate within you. Just now, it will be more recognizable and fill you with joy and inspiration. It will feel easier, because at a cellular level you can embody more Light, and Light is a powerful creational energy, as well as a healing energy.

You have gone through many phases of healing, and even though for some there may be more of that, for many of you it is now time to embrace the creational energy with a greater awareness of how much support you have from many Light Beings both on your Earth and in the other dimensions. One of the greatest things you will experience with this latest shift of energy is a more pronounced connection to that support, both from the seen and unseen realms. Take quiet time every day to tune in, to receive, *and* to emanate that supportive energy back out to those you are connected with, as well as to your world, and to the Universe—because you are a conduit. This latest shift has enabled you to be that conduit for the Light and the Love energy in a more effective way than ever possible, so just BE it and enjoy!

Messages of HOPE from "US" (United Souls of Heaven and Earth)

Energies Coursing Through Your Bodies
February 15, 2015

Dearest Beautiful Beings of Light,

Since our last message to you, and particularly in the past week or so, there has been an intensification of multidimensional energies coursing through your physical bodies (and through your minds). This intensification is highly beneficial to support the shift that we spoke of in our last message, though it can be not only uncomfortable, but physically painful. Please know, Dear Ones, that it is okay, that you are okay. Your bodies are just adjusting to the increased flow of these higher vibrational energies and the different frequencies that they bring to your Earth at this time.

Because so much is happening at once energetically, your body's response is to resist as the energies feel foreign, and thus sends out messages to fight them. As a result, it is creating joint pain and inflammation, muscle contractions and tension, headaches, heart palpitations, hot flashes, lethargy of your mind and Spirit, and a deep need to be alone. We encourage you to honour that by creating alone time in your own sacred space whenever possible to allow this most recent recalibration. Your bodies will adjust, and the more you honour and support it, the quicker that will happen. Also know, Dear Ones, that it is not just happening to *you*—it is happening to *all* humans. However, those of you who have given conscious choice to awaken and evolve are more sensitive to it in some ways, because you are fine-tuning your instrument (your mind and body), like an expensive violin, to send out a new sonic vibration to your world and to the Universe.

That new sonic vibration is that of harmony; your minds and bodies are in the orchestra pit warming up right now, and it feels and sounds discordant. As you continue to warm up and tune your instrument (your mind and body), you will align with your heart energy. You heart energy is like the conductor who comes in, raises their baton, and directs the beautiful symphony, the symphony of your personal life in harmonic concordance with Universal Life. That is quite a beautiful experience that your minds and bodies are preparing for now.

Notice we keep including your mind in our statements. Even though you may be extensively noticing the symptoms in your body right now, you are probably also aware of the chaos in your mind coming and going, having really clear and empowered thoughts, then all of a sudden shifting to chaotic, almost depressive thoughts. That is all part of the recalibration as well. So just be the witness, be the observer of what is happening with your thoughts (and emotions) without owning them or overly reacting to them, as that will allow them to clear with greater ease and efficiency.

As you know from your medical world, there is a greater awareness and use of Light therapy in healing the body and the mind, and that is what is happening on a Cosmic level for all of you; the more you allow and accept these emanations of high vibrational Light energy to move through your mind and body, even though it is uncomfortable and disorienting, the quicker you will feel the benefits of this most recent recalibration.

Messages of HOPE from "US" (United Souls of Heaven and Earth)

All of the influxes of Cosmic energy are to support your body, mind, Spirit, and heart to work in harmony with one another to create a joyful experience in your Earthly life, rather than the pattern of struggle that you have been entrenched in. Know that you have much support from all of your guides, angels and multi-dimensional beings at this time for this powerful shift, recalibration, and integration into your world. You are amazing Beings of Light on an incredible journey in a density-filled world to assist in Lightening it up at this time . . . and you are doing it! Give yourself a pat on the back and a special treat as the energy of LOVE is in the consciousness of humankind this weekend. Allow it to flow to you and through you!

Messages of HOPE from "US" (United Souls of Heaven and Earth)

The Light Stirs It Up!
March 15, 2015

Dearest Beautiful Beings of Light,

There have been many teachings from many Masters from the beginning of time about *Light*. We are referring to Light in an esoteric context, and an energy context, not just a technological context, though your technology is showing you what is possible with Light therapy. And what is happening now on your Earth is a greatly accelerated "Light therapy," both from within and from without, from above and from below. The Light illuminates, whether it is from a technological source or a Cosmic source, and when things are illuminated they get stirred up, shaken up, and transformed.

That is what is happening on your Earth right now, as well as within your bodies. Your scientists are making great breakthroughs in quantum physics and understanding the power of Light, not just in technology but with regard to the human DNA and all of its workings. The power you feel surging through your bodies of late is related to all of the upgrades that are happening on a Cosmic level to support the increase in knowledge, as well as transformation at a cellular level, in preparation for why you are really here on Earth—that is to be the conduit to anchor the higher vibrations and literally to *be* the Light! You have been told by many Masters that you are powerful beyond measure, and the most recent downloads of Light that you have received are stirring up the density and dissolving it. Though that process is still a challenging one for the human body at this point, we assure you that will change.

As with any big, major upgrade, whether it be in your house or your body, the power needs to be turned off for the renovation to be completed successfully before the power can be turned back on and all the great changes are lit up. The process of upgrading and rewiring has been extensive and ongoing for so long, for so many Light Beings on Earth, that it has become wearing and frustrating. This recent blast of solar flares this week has left many of you feeling incapacitated, but your being incapacitated is far from the truth. Yes, you have felt like your brain was turned off (and it was), and like your body was being burned out (and it was—the old density, that is), and that your emotions were being stirred up (and they were, because they were being cleared out). So much happening at once makes everyday life more challenging, though the benefits will be astounding as you will soon feel the Lightness from within. You will have a mind that works with unprecedented clarity, and a body that feels energized, *and* a greater connection to all that is.

Remember, Light illuminates so you can be more aware of what is really in your mind and consciousness, and can keep what is serving you and release what is not. Light transforms; it is a high-intensity, alchemical process that can create something totally different from what it was directed at, i.e., lead to gold. You have been like lead that is now under a high-intensity Light laser being transformed molecule by molecule to gold—solid, beautiful, and very, very valuable. Know that there is a profound reason for all of the issues that are coming up for you mentally, physically, emotionally, and spiritually. You are being transformed at a cellular level and will never be the same again. It is a wondrous and beautiful process if you will allow yourself to embrace it with an open mind and an open heart, having compassion for yourself and for all others who are also being stirred up by the *Light*!

Messages of HOPE from "US" (United Souls of Heaven and Earth)

Holding Your Light in Your New Reality
April 15, 2015

Dearest Beautiful Beings of Light,

There have been great shifts in energy on your Earth these past few months and, as a result, it has created a profound shift in reality for many human beings. That shift in reality is a direct consequence of the amount of *Light* that each of you is now able to hold within your physical being. It has been an intense process of the clearing and dissolving of the density within your physical realms. Your bodies have undergone powerful transformations at a cellular level to come to this point of truly being able to hold more Light within your physical body, and most importantly to reflect it back out. This reflecting of your Light projects a whole new reality, which you are now becoming more and more aware of. It is like showing a new movie on the screen of your awareness.

This new reality is being illuminated bit by bit, experience by experience to allow you to acclimatize to it as it is of a much higher vibration than you have experienced to date. Your body, and especially your mind, need time to adjust and accept this new reality that not only is being shown to you, but that you are actually creating. You are beginning to realize how powerful you are as creator beings, and through this latest level of energetic upgrade, you are now seeing the tangible results show up in your physical world, not just your spiritual awareness. This is due to the sheer numbers of humans now that are ready, willing, and able (and have given great intent for many years) to live in a world where you are truly accepted for who you are—not just in gender, race, colour, or creed, but for the Light Being that knows how to be in peace, harmony, joy, and love, because it is innate within you. It is coded into your cells and you are now ready to accept the truth of who you are.

The Light that is now emanating from you (whether you are aware of it or not) is beyond what was felt by many as possible on a mass level. There have always been the few special beings on your Earth—sages, emissaries, gurus, Masters that were very aware that holding Light was their purpose on Earth. Now it is not just the few chosen ones—it is *all* human beings. You all hold the codes in your cellular memory, and they are being activated by your intent for a better world, by your intent for serving others, by your intent to be the Light.

So it is with great joy that we tell you that you *are* doing it! There are so many of you that are being purposely intentional that this has created a contagion effect for those that may not have even thought of it. By you giving intention to truly hold your Light in all situations, it automatically transfers that energy to all involved. The New Reality you are creating by doing this will show up in ways you could never have imagined possible. Share your experiences of the Light with others; it will serve as confirmation for them that it truly is their New Reality, and that much has shifted for them and for your world.

Messages of HOPE from "US" (United Souls of Heaven and Earth)

Acclimatizing to Higher Frequency Energies
May 15, 2015

Dearest Beautiful Beings of Light,

You are in a period of acclimatizing to the many downloads of light that have recently been received by your Earth and your physical bodies, so it is important that you allow the integration to happen. Your bodies in particular need to get used to these higher frequencies. Your mind needs to get used to these new realities. Your emotions need to get used to the immensity of the energy that your heart can hold and, at the same time, emanate. If you are feeling exhausted and like you are not in control of your mind and emotions, that is why, Dear Ones.

Know also that you are always able to manage the energy; even though it seems new to you, it is actually *not* new—it is the coming forth of what you already know, and who you always have been as a Being of Light whose physical form is just catching up now! Soon it will all feel very familiar, and you will have a lot less doubts, questions and, yes, fewer fears. What is being activated for you at that deep, core, cellular level will allow you to not just let go of old dense energy and emotions, but to actually bypass them. You are already having many experiences of this—experiences that feel neutral, even though they may have felt quite dramatic for you in recent past. That is because in the higher frequency energies you have more access to your knowing, to your wisdom, to your peace, and to your love.

As you choose consciousness for yourself, it supports and facilitates the acclimatization' process. As you intentionally align with the higher frequency energies, you are the beacon for many others to do so as well, even if they do not have an intellectual understanding of what that is. It will just feel good and will automatically align for them, because you have embraced the process so willingly and with enthusiasm. You will notice as you maneuver any bumps that may show up for you that your relationships will actually take on a greater ease and acknowledgement of your truth, as well as theirs.

One of the things that will create the ease that you so desire through this acclimatization process is acceptance of where you are at in it, where others are at in it, and how they are showing up. There are many paths to harmonizing from within, and it is an incredible journey that each and every one of you have undertaken to be on Earth at this time of the Great Shift. When you accept what is happening, you change the vibration to allow the shift in energy to occur on higher (and deeper) levels. When you resist what is happening for yourself or others, you slow the shift that was aligning for the greater good of all.

Being in a place of knowing that all is well will quickly bring in the higher frequency energies that you will align with to sustain yourselves and your Earth in the new reality of peace and harmony, joy, and love. It has already been created, Dear Ones. Just let it in.

Messages of HOPE from "US" (United Souls of Heaven and Earth)

Energetic Adjustments Being Made

June 15, 2015

Dearest Beautiful Beings of Light,

In our last message to you we talked about acclimatizing to the higher frequencies, and now we want to assure you that there are many adjustments being made both by you, and for you, through this acclimatizing process. When something of lower density moves to a higher frequency, many things happen on different levels that are not yet understood by humans, so there is much dimensional unseen support for this to take place. It is a recalibration process that is becoming more recognized at the quantum level than ever before. In this recognition and acceptance there is much knowledge to be shared.

The adjustments are happening on all levels, and for everyone and everything. We say *everything* because it includes more than just your human biology. It affects everything in the Universe on a molecular level, every animate and inanimate object. Molecules are rearranging themselves even in the rocks, which you may not consider to be a living thing; however, everything in the Universe is comprised of energy and therefore is undergoing the same shifts, transformations, and adjustments at the level that is required for the harmonization that is happening.

You may have noticed that you are more in tune with everything, including objects that you would not have noticed before. Even though this may feel unsettling, and possibly overwhelming, just know that it is all part of the shift into higher consciousness and will become more streamlined and integrated into your everyday way of being. It all just feels new, and maybe even weird, as you are questioning what you are feeling and sensing. It is a time now of embracing all that you are, and that is why many of you are in need of much quiet and alone time. It is an important part of the acclimatization to these higher frequencies, and it also allows the necessary adjustments in energy to occur.

With the coming of the Solstice next week, you have been in even deeper preparation to align with the new energies. We commend you for your willingness, your commitment, and for trusting your inner knowing that is guiding you to keep moving forward on your spiritual path. To seek help when needed, and to share with others your experiences, as it affirms that you are all experiencing great shifts in awareness that *are* supporting the good of all on your Earth! When what you share with another resonates with them, it creates a harmonic energy that reverberates out into the Universe, and is expanded upon with the possibility being created for even more resonance and more *harmony*, both from within and in your external world.

The energetic adjustments that are currently being made are strengthening that harmony from within, and as a result you will see and feel more harmony in your personal world, and in your global world. Stay in the knowing and the allowing of the amazing shifts you are creating for yourself and others. There is much joy to be gained.

Messages of HOPE from "US" (United Souls of Heaven and Earth)

Do You Believe in Unlimited Possibilities?
July 15, 2015

Dearest Beautiful Beings of Light,

This is a question that can take you to a place of great awareness and profound experiences, depending on how you answer it, and how much you open your consciousness to receiving the information that will create the experiences. The expansion that you are currently in is happening at such an accelerated pace that it sometimes becomes a blur in your mind. That is for a reason, Dear Ones. It is to keep you from over-thinking and analyzing everything too much.

Most of you can accept that there are many possibilities for you in your life, and are even getting more comfortable that they can be beneficial possibilities; however, now is a time when the possibilities are unlimited. Everything that you experience is only limited by your thought process and your willingness to see the bigger picture, even if you cannot yet imagine what that would be exactly. You actually do not have a context yet in which to put those experiences, and that is what is rapidly shifting for you. With all of the self-help, self-growth, new thought, and spiritual seeking that your past few generations have been doing, it has not only opened your minds and healed your emotions, but has expanded your consciousness to receive more awareness of what is beyond the 3D physical experience.

This awareness is now showing you in great leaps and bounds what is possible for you as individuals, and more importantly, as a human race evolving . . . making more conscious choices. With each conscious choice you open to more power from within and more support from the Universe. As these energies work hand in hand, the possibilities for yourself, personally and for your world, multiply exponentially until you truly see that you are limitless. The only limits that you have are what you are placing on yourself (or allowing others to place on you). It is a time of win/win on your Earth. There does not have to be a winner and a loser in any situation. In the New Energy that is available to all on your Earth, you can choose to rise above what has kept you in fear, and therefore limited. You can start to experience grander visions that you never would have thought possible before, because you are now attuned to them.

With the many, many energetic shifts that you have endured over the past few years you will now start to truly see, feel, and experience why they had to happen. You have been in preparation and are now ready to accept the unlimited possibilities, whereas before that would have been overwhelming, or not even on your scope of reality. Now your scope of reality is greatly expanded so that you can embrace possibilities that will seem like miracles, though really are just your New Normal way of being in the world. It is an exciting time that you have chosen to live in to bring so many possibilities through into your everyday experience.

As you read our words, know that you are forerunners in anchoring the Light on your Earth to illuminate for *all* to see, and *feel* what is possible to create for themselves and your world with so many possibilities of beneficial outcome. Keep your focus and intention on these words and you will be amazed at what happens. You are ready!

Messages of HOPE from "US" (United Souls of Heaven and Earth)

More Light Coming to Your Earth

August 15, 2015

Dearest Beautiful Beings of Light,

In the weeks and months to come there is more Light coming to Earth than humanity has yet to experience. It is possible because of all of the intentional, as well as the oblivious, awakening that has happened on your Earth. You have cleared so much density that you are more open conduits for the Light to filter through to your Earth and all Her beings.

We have spoken many times about human beings being the receptacles and conduits for anchoring Light through your physical bodies and all the challenges that are presented because of that. Now you will truly be able to experience the results and benefits of having done that for so many decades now. It can be likened to erosion: you cannot notice the effects of a few drops of water on a rock, though consistent and ongoing drops on the rock over a period of time will show you a result. And that is what has been happening with the anchoring of Light on Earth: you will now see the results of that consistency that so many of you have dedicated yourself to through your spiritual seeking that has led, for many of you, to careers that support others as they embrace their own awakening to the Light within them, and within others.

So as that becomes the New Normal, you are now able to embody more Light, not just within the cells of your physical being, but within the mind as well. There have been many upgrades within your brain to receive higher vibrational energy, and that means you have a greater capacity to understand what is happening, though now you have the language and opportunities to share your experience, knowledge and services to those ready to receive on a more conscious level.

Therefore, as this Light energy is in flow to you, through you, and from you more freely with greater ease, grace, and confidence, there will be more Light energy coming to Earth to support you. It is like the volume can now be turned up because you have adjusted and acclimatized to the higher vibrational energies. It is a profound time in the evolution of humanity from density to Light, and the rest of this year will give you tangible examples of just how profound. Many of you already are experiencing the effects—for example, in family relationship healings, increases in abundance and health, starting to live the life you have always wanted; now you can create all of that, and more, with greater ease.

There is more to come, Dear Ones, as you have surpassed so many hurdles and blocks to accessing the truths of the Universe, the truths of who you are, and the awareness of the Light—the Light that you are, always have been and always will be as an energetic expression in the human existence that you have chosen to experience as part of the Great Shift. We honour you and support you as the magnificent Light Being that you already are!

Messages of HOPE from "US" (United Souls of Heaven and Earth)

New Vistas Are Arising
September 15, 2015

Dearest Beautiful Beings of Light,

Out of the quagmire of muck, pain, chaos, and uncertainty there is a steady, ever-increasing rise of something new and wonderful pushing its way to the surface of your awareness, to the surface of your consciousness, and to the surface of your physical sight and experiences on your Earth. It has been slow to rise, and now will take on a more accelerated trajectory of exposure to you. It is new to you in this incarnation, as well as being remembered from innate knowings from beyond this life.

The vistas that are arising for you now are panoramic, enabling you to see (and feel) in *all* directions, in *all* things and situations, the gifts and the profoundness of each of your experiences to this point. It is the welling up—the rising up—of a greater knowing that its time has come, and that time is now! As you experience the Cosmic alignments of this month in particular, be willing to see the pleasing vistas in your life, and in your memory, as that is what is being activated now. There has been an incredible amount of clearing at a mass consciousness level (and is still ongoing for some); the view has cleared, the clouds have lifted off the horizon to show you what is *really* there—not what you perceived because of what you have been told and conditioned to.

You have the opportunity to see, and to feel (we keep emphasizing the words *to feel* as that is the way you are able to *see*, whether it is in your inner vision or in an outward sight through your physical eyes) the changes that *have* come! Not just the ones you have hoped for, prayed for, begged for, and stomped your feet for, but the changes that you have manifested, the ones you have created through your intentions, through your dedication to your Light path and serving the world, and through your honouring of yourself as a Light Being.

You are now looking more and more through the eyes of love, through the eyes of compassion, and feeling the depths of knowing that new, lighter experiences are possible in your life now. The density, the darkness, the heaviness have served their purpose in showing you what you do not want, and empowering you to focus all your energy—body, mind, spirit, and heart—on what you do want, and now you are seeing those desires created right before your eyes. Keep your eye on the creational ball, Dear Ones, as it is the one that is serving you now as the rest disintegrates from your experience, like the pixels in an electronic picture just becoming less and less until there is no picture, or vista in that which has kept you encumbered.

You have great ability and capacity to create whatever it is you so desire that is in the greatest interest of the whole. Many powerful energies and forces have aligned at this time to support your creating from that new vista that you are seeing (and feeling) of beauty, harmony, abundance, peace and love. It truly is what you can create, because you can see the picture in your mind—and, more importantly, feel it in your heart! Know that it is done!

Messages of HOPE from "US" (United Souls of Heaven and Earth)

Standing on Higher Ground
October 15, 2015

Dearest Beautiful Beings of Light,

As you are now on the other side (for now) of the powerful Cosmic and astrological alignments and energetic eruptions of late, you literally *are* standing on higher ground energetically. You can liken it to the eruption of a volcano in the ocean. It has been happening underwater, so it may not have been able to be seen, but surely it can be felt; then the heat and lava and ash rise to the surface and start to form new land masses that you can eventually stand upon and find something solid to walk upon again. That is what has happened energetically, and you are not sure if it is really safe to walk upon or even real. We assure you, it is.

You are truly on higher ground metaphorically, and physically able to see in a 360-degree rotation of all that has happened and what is presently being shown to you. You have a much farther-reaching vision with your physical eyes, as well as your internal eye, to see, feel and to understand what is happening, thus allowing you the capability to negotiate your maneuvers in this new unfamiliar terrain. It is like traveling to a new country that you have never been to before and needing to get your orientation and to learn the customs and way of life. On the higher ground, on which you now stand, you get to create the customs and way of being that will serve you. That, of course, will ultimately serve the whole.

Pay attention, Dear Ones, to what you are seeing in this New World that you have entered; feel the energy with more than just your five physical senses. Allow yourself to go beyond what you know and are comfortable with. Much will be visible from this higher ground, tangibly in your personal life and energetically in your spiritual life. You are anchoring the higher way of being that we spoke of in an earlier transmission, and it is moment, by moment, by moment, choice, by choice, by choice. What you will experience as you stay in the moment is greater access to your own personal higher way of being that supports your journey, which ultimately does support those around you that you care deeply about, even if they are not quite yet on the same ground that you are on, or seeing what you are seeing. They will get it by osmosis by you just *being* it, by you *living* it.

The *it* is whatever you make of it, so we encourage you to lift your eyes, and to lift your heart out of the density, out of the quagmires of situations, to see, feel, embody, and anchor the higher vibrations that are increasingly available to you now just by thought. Then, when you add the word and the action to that higher vibrational thought, you truly create miracles in your life as well as in the lives of others. Do not be awed by what unfolds in your life, as it is the New Normal and your innate way of being that you are just coming to recognize and to accept. As you accept that you are already there (whatever that means for you), then you are. It is done, so be it! Enjoy what shows up for you now and share it with others.

… *Messages of HOPE from "US" (United Souls of Heaven and Earth)*

Your Perceptions Are Changing
November 15, 2015

Dearest Beautiful Beings of Light,

Have you noticed that what you are seeing and experiencing in your lives and in the world feels different? Do you feel that you are looking at things differently, possibly more often now from a higher perspective? There is a reason for that, Dear Ones. You truly are standing on higher ground as we shared with you in our last message. You are able to perceive things from a brand new way of being that then ultimately gives you a whole new perspective of people and situations that is not as bogged down with judgement and criticism.

This is all because of the immense clearings and transformations you have gone through to literally lighten your Spirit to shift into higher vibrational energy. It is from this place you now stand in energetically that your perceptions of people and events can also now shift to a view that supports the whole of humanity, rather than segregates it or diminishes certain aspects of human expression. And one of the greatest perceptions that has shifted and is having the most profound effect is your perception of yourself, and a deeper acceptance of not only who you are as a Spirit in human form, but the power that you have within you to see the magnificence in everyone and everything. As you embrace that power, you are instrumental in the shift, not only of the circumstances in your personal life but of world events and their effect on the Universal unfolding of the connectedness of all things.

These changes in perception are easing the stress you experience in your life, as well as inspiring yourself and others to allow even more expansion of awareness and opening of your heart. When you see (and feel) the bigger picture, you then become part of the unfoldment, just through your knowing and sharing that knowing with others. Take time to note how things feel different, how you are thinking differently; bring it into the tangible form for confirmation for your mind, as it is not your mind that is perceiving. It is your heart that then sends the information to your mind. It then bypasses ego to become a thought that is more encompassing of the *All* and the Unity of the Universe and all Her beings.

It is a wonderful trajectory that you are on, with much powerful awareness that will just appear for you to know that what is happening is real. It is tangible and it is livable, right here on Earth, right through your own lives and the expression of your Divine Essence in this realm of density—the density that is shifting ever so quickly to become the Garden of Eden that it was always meant to be. Let your new perceptions of everything show you what is possible. There are many of you now that are able to hold a high enough vibration to have the 360-degree view that we shared with you in our last message. You are joining your magnificent Light energies to illuminate these perceptions for all to see and feel! It is a wondrous place to stand and view, and we support your being there.

Messages of HOPE from "US" (United Souls of Heaven and Earth)

Wrap Up 2015 with Love, Embrace 2016 with Joy!

December 15, 2015

Dearest Beautiful Beings of Light,

The title of our message to you this day sounds simple enough, and is even appropriate for this season of sacred holidays and celebrating the New Year to come. However, we would like to put a sacred spin on these words so there not only is more meaning to them, but more application and more recognition of these words as you move from this magnanimous year of changes to 2016, with all of its incredible possibilities!

As you wrap each gift that you are preparing to give to another, imagine it being wrapped in the energy of *love*. Now you may say to yourself, *Well, I already do that! That is why I bought the gift in the first place.* So we say to you, *Make it bigger, farther reaching, all-encompassing, covering all aspects of everyone and everything!* All it takes is intent, and as you intend to wrap yourself and everyone and everything in the energy of *love*, you will automatically step over the threshold of this transformative year of 2015 into the frequency of JOY for 2016.

2016 adds up to 9, which is about completion and wisdom. As you allow the completion of the cycles or circumstances that you may have been in that might have felt challenging or difficult, you will feel the wisdom rise to the surface of your consciousness. The wisdom is revealed because you have acknowledged your truth and your own power to shift from within, the strength to know what to do, and the willingness to take the actions. As you acknowledge that in yourself, you lift much weight and density out of energy fields—yours and well as that of many others. As that density disperses, there is *so* much more room available for joy! And who does not want more joy in their life? How good does it feel to see more joy in other's lives? All you have to do is to intend it, and embrace it with all your heart.

2015 was an incredible year of heart-opening, not just for those on a spiritual path—though for many who did not even know they were ready to open their hearts. Whether through crisis, or powerful intention, it *is* happening. Recognize it, acknowledge it, and embrace the energy of *joy* that goes hand-in-hand with making choices from the heart, making choices from *love*. That is how we change the world. JOY to the world and all her peoples this beautiful season of giving and receiving the energy of *love*!

Epilogue

As of the publication of these life-changing messages from the first half of the DECADE OF LIGHT 2010–2020, we have just come through the year 2016, which carries the vibration of 9 in numerology. 9 is about completion and the wisdom that hopefully accompanies any completions that you may have orchestrated for yourself, or that Spirit has orchestrated for our world and the Universe we are connected to. 2016 will go down in history as one of the most chaotic, surprising, and intense years in the history of humankind to date because of the vast amounts of photonic Light that our bodies were able to process. The photonic Light emanations from the Universe created an alchemical process for all those on Earth that was physically uncomfortable, emotionally and mentally depleting, and yet at the same time spiritually enlightening. This enabled us to shift our thoughts and beliefs about ourselves and others to a way of being that was much more loving and compassionate, to see the drastic contrasts, to bless them and shift the energy for our way of perceiving them. The shifts, changes, and upheavals were opening our hearts and our consciousness in preparation for us to step into 2017 with a more empowered way of being. We were acting upon our deep spiritual knowing that could no longer be denied.

In numerology, 2017 adds up to 1, which carries the energy of new beginnings, the start of a new cycle, an opportunity to create something brand new! It is with great excitement that I look forward to this year, embracing all of the incredible upgrades in frequency and vibration that have come through our physical bodies to support us in this magnificent creational energy.

Make sure to get on our newsletter list at www.judithonley.com for notification of the publishing of VOLUME 2 of these beautiful messages that "US" will be giving humanity in the second half of the DECADE OF LIGHT 2016–2020. It will be published in early 2021!

Messages of HOPE from "US" (United Souls of Heaven and Earth)

Acknowledgements

To all those who have supported me and believed in my journey, even when I doubted the magnificence of what was happening to me, I give my most heartfelt thanks and appreciation. To name a few: Susan Painter and Susan Sparkes, who were my first "channelees"; Kevin Nelson, for his beautiful musical accompaniment during the early days of my group channels in Toronto; Barbara Lupton, who gave support in so many ways while I was traveling and connecting with like-hearted people; Yasmin Viranni, who also spread the word far and wide through her networks of what I was doing; Rev. Maryum Morse at the Centre of the Heart Church in Santa Barbara, California; Liz Ryan at Gateway 2 Ranch in Kamloops, British Columbia; Brian and Annette Olynek at Quantum Leaps Retreat Centre in Golden, British Columbia; Mary Wileichuk at Akasha's Den in Oakville, Ontario; Madeleine Marentette at Grail Springs Retreat Centre in Bancroft, Ontario; Monste Bastus at Centro el Manantial Retreat Centre in Santes Creus, Spain; Daisy Foss at Daisy Centres Healing Retreat, Glastonbury, England; Shirling Kao at Jade Wellness Studio, Sault Ste. Marie, Ontario; and to the many other friends, colleagues, and acquaintances who are too many to mention who have hosted me in their homes, clinics or retreat centres, helped organize gatherings and events, or just showed up because they knew they were meant to be there. Bless you for listening to your knowing.

through Judith Onley

Special mention to Kelly McCormick and Mark Daniel for providing emotional and energetic support and guidance when I needed it many times throughout this metaphysical adventure; to Jen Clarke for proofreading and admin support; and especially to Julie Heyman for mentoring me unwaveringly along this incredible journey, as well as for her editing skills and talents. She has been my cheerleader, as well as my voice of reason in so many situations. I am eternally grateful to call her my friend and colleague.

About The Author

Judith Onley is a Spiritual Mentor and Channel who communicates and teaches with the assistance and wisdom of "US" (United Souls of Heaven and Earth), a group of non-physical spiritual teachers whose purpose in coming forth at this time is "*to activate the Divine Essence within all Human Beings.*"

She shares this empowering information live in group settings, via international teleconferences, as well as with individual clients. Those who attend group channels are profoundly affected, not only by the words of the messages, but by the energy, as they actually receive an activation at a deep cellular level. Word of these Divine messages has spread, and Judith has been traveling and teaching throughout North America, Mexico, Spain, Morocco and England, sharing the loving energy and empowering messages for the benefit of all those who are awakening at this time of unprecedented shifts, transformations, and possibilities on Planet Earth.

Judith is also a mother and a grandmother. She lives in Canada and is currently writing a number of other books. She cherishes the opportunity to share her life experiences to inspire and motivate people. She brings "Spirit into Being" by offering programs and consultations that facilitate the complete integration of Body, Mind, Spirit, and Heart. Her books on these messages are available in both full-size and booklet form to enable you to access the energy and wisdom of "US" for yourself at any time.

Receive Cosmic energy updates, as well as energetic transmissions and activations, by joining Judith and "US" on their bi-monthly "DECADE OF LIGHT" teleconference live channels. The messages (and energetic transmissions in this book) are a product of the first five years of this Decade of incredible downloads of Light through the human body. Be part of a growing awakening community of Light Beings and Way-showers that know they are here on Earth to anchor Light to illuminate the path for others.

Judith offers private Spiritual Mentoring sessions, Group Channelling sessions, and a wide range of Spiritual Self-Development classes and workshops online and in person. Receive lots of great information and inspirational support by subscribing to Judith's monthly newsletter.

Visit www.judithonley.com to sign up for Judith's informative and inspiring newsletter, and for more details on the telechannels, ordering books, Mp3 recordings of channels, and booking private mentoring sessions. Any enquiries for booking Judith for interviews, presentations, or for hosting live group channels can be done through her website.

Messages of HOPE from "US" (United Souls of Heaven and Earth)

You can also order the following books on Judith's website:

KEY POINTS booklet version of *Messages of HOPE from "US" (United Souls of Heaven and Earth) Decade of Light—Volume 1*

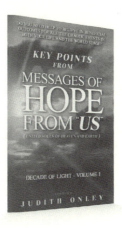

Your Mastery - Live It Now! softcover and KEY POINTS booklet version

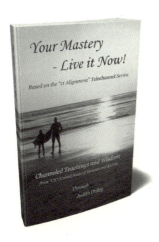

Printed in Canada